ENDORSEMEN

It is my privilege to acknowledge Oabona's extraordinary story, which exemplifies the principles of Exponential Organizations. By aligning his entrepreneurial journey with a Massive Transformative Purpose, he has shown how resilience, happiness, and present-focused leadership can inspire others to create lasting impact. This book is a testament to how exponential thinking can transform not only businesses but also communities and lives.

Salim Ismail
Founder and CEO OpenExo
Former Vice President of Innovation at Yahoo
Author of *Exponential Organizations*

Oabona Kgengwenyane's book is a heartfelt celebration of the indomitable spirit of African entrepreneurs. It captures the resilience, creativity, and boldness needed to overcome challenges and seize opportunities unique to our continent. As an entrepreneur in one of Africa's self-developed retail chains, I deeply resonate with his vision of leveraging innovation and resilience to drive growth in our continent. This inspiring work reignites the belief that Africa's greatness lies in the power of its people to dream and deliver.

Ramachandran Ottapathu
Founder and CEO of Listed Choppies Group, Regional
Supermarket Company

If we do not think for ourselves, we place our future in the hands of others—it is up to us to create our own new world. Political freedom is meaningless if we are not going to use it to fundamentally transform the economic system that excluded black people from the economic mainstream and main streets. And if we do not handle our freedom well, the colonisers will come back as investors. We must intentionally address the fact that we are the only African country that became free from colonialism and did not exponentially increase the education levels of our people, and increase, by at least double digits, the ownership of the economy by our people.

Professor Bonang Mohale
Chancellor: University of the Free State, South Africa

Oabona Kgengwenyane is a true visionary—an entrepreneur, engineer, farmer, and thought leader who embodies the resilience and innovative spirit of African entrepreneurship. His journey, rooted in Botswana's rich heritage and shaped by personal and professional triumphs, is nothing short of inspiring.

Having engaged with Oabona multiple times on the Mogobe Nuggets of Wisdom Podcast and welcomed him as a guest speaker to my Entrepreneurship Mentorship Program, I have seen firsthand his passion for transformation and his commitment to empowering the next generation of business leaders. His insights have left a lasting impact on my mentees, pushing them to think bigger, embrace resilience, and take bold steps in their entrepreneurial journeys.

In *INNOLEAD: The Inner Game of African Entrepreneurship*, Oabona shares deep insights on endurance, happiness, and the power of living in the present. He masterfully weaves his personal experiences with practical wisdom, offering entrepreneurs a roadmap to success that goes beyond wealth—one that embraces purpose, well-being, and the transformative impact of business on society.

This book is a must-read for any aspiring entrepreneur, business leader, or changemaker looking to build something meaningful in Africa and beyond. Oabona's story is proof that with resilience, vision, and a commitment to continuous growth, ordinary people can achieve extraordinary success.

Mompoloki Lerumo Mogobe
Entrepreneur | Investor | Speaker/Author
Host of *Mogobe Nuggets of Wisdom* Podcast
MD of Mogobe Inc Group of Companies

This book by Oabona is a true and honest reflection of something much bigger than he initially imagined. His journey is also the journey of the Batswana and their country, Botswana—and the African continent!

This book is a dream-catcher and vision creator for each African, every family, and every team that is building a better society. Healthy societies that can use their resilience and vision to address their challenges.

More than that, this book is a roadmap for African leaders, their creative countries, and their happy followers, a book of work and the growth of our continental economy—in this, the African century.

Dr. Coetzee Bester
University of Pretoria, South Africa

INNOLEAD: The Inner Game of African Entrepreneurship" is a powerful testament to resilience, passion, and purpose. Oabona's story is not just about overcoming adversity—it is a roadmap for redefining success through optimism, balance, and impact. His philosophy of *EntreHappiness* reminds us that entrepreneurship is not just about profit but about joy, purpose, and transformation.

With deep wisdom and heartfelt storytelling, Oabona inspires us to embrace The Gift of Resilience, The Gift of Happiness, and The Gift of Now, turning challenges into opportunities and living fully in the present. This book is a beacon of hope, a love letter to Africa, and a call to action for those who dare to dream and build a legacy.

A must-read for anyone seeking to lead with soul and heart. Thank you, Oabona.

Joaquin Serra
Senior Vice President and Chief Business Development Officer at
Natura Bissé Barcelona, Spain

I have known Oabona when we were still young engineers at Debswana Diamond Company. Mike, as we called him then, was highly invested in the company and applied himself fully to his work. Mike challenged the status quo, recommended changes to ways of work, and was resented by seniors for his tenacity and inquisitive mind. Later on, after leaving Debswana, he formed Xpert Botswana, a project management firm. I worked with Xpert Botswana when they became an implementation partner for the highly successful Debswana 5-Year North Star Strategy programme. Mike's diligence, tenacity, and purposefulness soon positioned him as one of Botswana's great entrepreneurial minds, with multiple businesses to his name. Today, he stands out as an inspiration and a champion of "EntreHappiness," the term he coined to describe entrepreneurs who embrace happiness and joy. He is practicing the words of biblical Solomon, who said: "The blessing of the LORD makes one rich, and He adds no sorrow with it." (Proverbs 10:22 NKJV). Oabona, may you continue prospering in your chosen path, and inspire a new generation of happy and joyful entrepreneurs, who are excited to serve our country, Africa and the world!

Balisi Mohumi Bonyongo
Board Chairperson, First National Bank Botswana
Former Managing Director, Debswana Diamond Company
Gaborone, Botswana

This is a thinker's book. By sharing lessons he has learnt from his life's journey, Oabona's writing reminds us that we lead ourselves first, and only if capable of self-leadership can we lead others. In this publication, Oabona shares useful lessons, many of which should resonate with the readers while offering useful points of reference for those of us who occasionally take stock of our entrepreneurial, professional, or personal lives.

Sheila Khama
Non-Executive Director- All Current, FTSE and
NASDAQ listed entities
Former CEO, De Beers Botswana

I have known Oabona for many years, and for me, he is the real personification of the expression "taking the bull by the horns." His life experience is certainly a journey worth learning from, a journey of not accepting your limitations, but aiming for the furthest star.

Dumelang Saleshando
Member of Parliament, Maun North
Leader of Opposition, Botswana Parliament

We are fortunate to have observed Oabona from close proximity for close to 40 years and can attest to his commitment to achieving excellence, whether it was as a tennis player, a scholar, an entrepreneur, a family man, or indeed a friend. Armed with a global perspective, he is a patriot with a passion for "seeing his country do (much) better," which is not only inspirational, it is infectious. We often ask him, "Why do you bother? Who, after all, in the country, is listening?" In truth, we all need to listen (and, more importantly, ACT thereafter)—and that is why this book is not only important, it is essential.

**Dr N. Ndwapi, T. Matthews, S. Matlala,
D Reetsang, Dr M. Matsheka, Dr M. Sento**
Close Friends

True success doesn't begin with strategy—it begins with soul. In *INNOLEAD*, Oabona Michael Kgengwenyane invites entrepreneurs on a powerful journey inward. This book is more than business advice—it's a blueprint for inner alignment, outer impact, and lasting joy. If you're ready to build a business without losing yourself in the process, this is your guide.

Dr. Kary Oberbrunner
CEO of Igniting Souls and Instant IP
USA Today and *Wall Street Journal* Bestselling Author

INNOLEAD

Unpacking the Inner Game of African Entrepreneurship

INNOLEAD

*Unpacking the Inner Game of
African Entrepreneurship*

OABONA KGENGWENYANE

ethos
collective

Printed in the United States of America

Published by Igniting Souls
PO Box 43, Powell, OH 43065
IgnitingSouls.com

LCCN: 2024906581
Paperback ISBN: 978-1-63680-277-0
Hardback ISBN: 978-1-63680-278-7
eBook ISBN: 978-1-63680-279-4

Available in paperback, hardcover, e-book, and audiobook.

Any Internet addresses (websites, blogs, etc.) and telephone numbers printed in this book are offered as a resource. They are not intended in any way to be or imply an endorsement by Igniting Souls, nor does Igniting Souls vouch for the content of these sites and numbers for the life of this book.

Some names and identifying details may have been changed to protect the privacy of individuals.

Dedication

To my late mother Mma Mmiga,
who taught me grit and human connections.
To my wife Nancy, who taught me companionship.
To my children and grandkids, who reinforce my life.

CONTENTS

PART ONE: THE GIFT OF ENDURANCE

PART THREE: THE GIFT OF NOW

FOREWORD

BY GARY MOTTERSHEAD

Oabona's commitment to his own growth and desire to help others were clearly evident from the first day I met him at a Strategic Coach workshop in Toronto. I was incredibly impressed that someone would travel all the way from Botswana to attend workshops in Canada. My feeling then was that this man is very special! When I have the opportunity to be his coach, I am always grateful for the insights he brings into the room.

Oabona's book, *Innolead*, is further evidence of his personal commitment to helping others. You would never know upon meeting Oabona that he has overcome hardships and obstacles that those of us in the West could never imagine. The road to being an entrepreneur, let alone a highly successful one, growing up in Botswana, is more like "work-hardened" metal. The more it is hit, the harder it becomes.

What's important for all of us is not just the resilience that Oabona has demonstrated but the concepts of Entrehappiness and JoyReP that he shares and lives by. The principles behind these two concepts enabled Oabona to transform from a 30-something high-achieving workaholic to a more purposeful, impactful, and happy Oabona.

Oabona shares his life, the ups and the downs, in a way that inspires and encourages us to transform our lives for the better, not just for ourselves but for all we touch.

Gary Mottershead
Founder of GCP Industrial Products, Coach at Strategic Coach®
Author of *Nimble Future*, Host of *Clarity Generates Confidence* Podcast

INTRODUCTION

THE INNER GAME OF AFRICAN ENTREPRENEURSHIP

I speak of Africa and golden joys.
—Shakespeare

The tree on the cover of this book is a camel thorn tree, an indigenous African tree renowned for its longevity and shade. Its nutritious pods give life as they feed cattle, goats, and sheep.

Of all the trees on my farm, this one is the most majestic, spreading its branches like an umbrella, ready to protect lives from the occasional scorching African sun heat. It sticks out in the African bushveld open landscapes as if saying, "I lead around here through nourishing the land."

In many ways, this tree represents what I strive to be in my life. Its longevity reminds me of the endurance I cultivated in my childhood, and, like this tree, it gives shade and food to anyone who may need it. I want to give you the nourishment you need to thrive and find happiness.

When you have passion for life, you're energized, enthused, and optimistic. As a young boy growing up with an abusive father and a single mother, I learned to navigate my way from village life in Botswana to becoming a successful entrepreneur.

I am the founder of Innolead Consulting, DigitalGae Technologies, and Manenzo Farming, a group I have led for a quarter of a century. This work is not just about running a business; it represents my refuge for creativity and happiness.

After decades of experience, I have so much to offer humanity: more relationships to enjoy, areas to explore, and fun activities to try. I wish this for everyone, especially entrepreneurs in Africa, where we have an abundance of challenges to solve for our people. We must emancipate our people from poverty and strife so we can pursue long-lasting happiness.

Now that I am in the second half of my life, I have transformed from what British psychologist Raymond Cattell called fluid intelligence (learning new information to solve problems) to crystalline intelligence (using existing information to solve problems). I use my 25 years working with clients to wise up, self-author my story, and live a life according to my terms. It has been so liberating, and I wanted to share it with you in this book.

I have evolved from a thirty-something high achiever named Michael to a more purposeful and impactful Oabona. I am very excited about what I can achieve as an entrepreneur, and I am focused, in particular, on advancing people's lives from poverty to a life of well-being and joy.

For over ten thousand years, Africa has aroused the interest of other nations due to the abundance of resources we've been endowed with. The Roman Empire relied on our grain supplies over three thousand years ago, countries resourced their development through African slavery, and Europeans exploited gold and ivory and later colonized our nations.

Despite having taken back our governing powers after decades of colonization, we still linger at the bottom of most development indicators. Worse still, we are losing the core humane aspects of our being. The essence of our survival over centuries is our "Ubuntu," which differentiates who we are and keeps us happy in the face of challenges. I'll talk more about that in Chapter Seven.

It's imperative that we do not lose our critical nutrients for well-being and happiness at the mercy of modernisation. As Robert J. Anderson and William A. Adams say in *Mastering Leadership*, the best leader is a "radical human," a person who embraces unity with others through vulnerability and love.

Happy, successful entrepreneurs who embrace my concepts of "EntreHappiness" and "JoyReP" are primarily creative leaders who love people.

In no way am I suggesting there is a magic formula for instant entrepreneurial happiness. The turns and toils still have to be experienced, including typical business challenges that draw on one's bio-psycho-social fitness.

My goal is to inspire people of all nations, especially those in the developing world and in Africa, where despair can sometimes overwhelm us and cause us to regress. The book is also for global readers and researchers who wish to appreciate the life of ordinary Africans.

I tell the story of an ordinary African entrepreneur in a country that just 55 years ago was classified as one of the poorest in the world.

I have divided this book into three essential sections: the gift of endurance, the gift of happiness, and the gift of now. As you will see, these have shaped who I am and how I have found success personally and professionally.

The Gift of Endurance

While doing metal work in high school, I learned that beating brass or copper with a mallet makes it "harden." In other words, stress and hammering make the metal sheets tougher.

After learning this, I reflected on the natural stress we often go through to make us more mature, resilient, and better performing. Like most entrepreneurs, I have had my "mallet hammer" beatings, and despite emotional turmoil, I have become a better person.

Over my 30-year career as an entrepreneur, I have experienced many low moments, but I've learned from both the ups and downs. I am not, by any means, a typical rockstar entrepreneur who has made millions of dollars. My story is about how the ordinary can become extraordinary. It is about how, despite humble beginnings, we can overcome obstacles to realize a fruitful, fulfilling life.

Even outside entrepreneurship, don't we all deserve that?

Entrepreneurs of any level can make a huge impact on the lives around us–from a Manenzo farm worker feeding his family by growing spinach for the first time in the arid sands of the Kgalagadi to a farm worker owning cows for the first time (a vital integrity matter in our society), a 40-year-old driver opening their first bank account, and a talented young Innolead consultant who supports her family and learns about living a more holistic life.

Such impact has made me steadfast over the years that entrepreneurs do not have to be headline personalities like South African billionaire Patrice Motsepe, Nigerian Aliko Dangote, Elon Musk, Jeff Bezos, or Richard Branson. Anyone can make a difference to society's less privileged in an impactful way.

One of my mottos throughout my life has been, "There is no gain without pain." The anchor of this philosophy was inspired by my mother, who went through a deeply abusive marriage for ten years before getting a divorce and single-handedly raising four successful children.

As her firstborn, I witnessed firsthand the abuse, how her strong religious beliefs helped her cope, and her steadfast nature while facing life's challenges. Her series of griefs and rebounds were right there in my face!

Through these challenging experiences, I stayed resilient and focused on what matters most to me. The difference between a successful person and an unsuccessful person is the ability to recognize hardships and not be overwhelmed.

The Stoic philosopher Ryan Holiday derived this quote from the Roman Emperor Marcus Aurelius: "The obstacle is the way." The obstacle "work hardens" us to withstand the ups and downs of our uncertain and troubled world.

My life of showing up has also contributed to the grit that has characterized my journey. My religious background defined my spiritual grounding, which still holds today, even if I am no longer a strong religious person (for now!).

Being a member of the Boy Scout movement reinforced these principles in me, and my active participation in sports and clubs throughout my younger years also built a thick skin.

In my life, momentous events have formed a pattern of dealing with low moments. Being an entrepreneur in Africa is no child's play; the terrain is rough, and the regulations and red tape can be stifling. My inner stronghold has been tested many times, and one time, I did think of quitting, but the urge for economic freedom and a bigger future kept me on the cause.

As the African saying goes, "letsema le thata ka mongaalone," which loosely translates to "Challenges are for the owner to own up to—the challenge is only as tough as you perceive it."

The Gift of Happiness

I have always been driven by my passion for life!

As Aristotle said 2,500 years ago, "Happiness is the meaning and goal of life, the whole aim and end of human existence."

Happiness is one of the most important concepts I have studied, so important that you will find its theme woven throughout my book, even outside the section dedicated to happiness.

All of us, regardless of income or country, need a happier world.

In 1985, Bob Geldof and Midge Ure organized an event to support the devastating famine in Ethiopia. Famous singers gathered to sing "We Are The World," a song that forever rings in my ears. The song promises that we can all contribute to a better world in our own unique ways. Entrepreneurs, as natural problem solvers, are best suited to this task.

I have mingled with entrepreneurs from the US, Canada, and Europe for eight years through the Strategic Coach® program in Canada. Take it from me: We think the same. The difference is our stifling environment and ecosystems in Africa, which limit the potential of millions of young entrepreneurs.

In life, we will face situations that trigger anger, anxiety, and disappointment. To be happy people, we need to accept that there will be unhappy moments.

My thirties were my lowest period as I struggled with start-up pressures and failures. A classic workaholic, I burned sixty to seventy hours a week at work, and by the time I got home, I was too exhausted to spend meaningful time with my family.

I was successful but not fully happy. Something was missing.

I had bought into the American culture of individualism and the "I can do it alone" approach. This overemphasis on self can be detrimental. We achieve through and with others. This is the African way, as captured by the African Tswana proverb *"se tshwarwa ke ntša pedi ga se thata,"* or "What is tackled by two dogs (vs. one) is much easier."

My forties were a turning point. The rugged individualist in me was spent, and I needed a paradigm shift.

The alternative would have been catastrophic (health and well-being) to me and the businesses I ran.

From owning a farm to becoming more health-conscious (thanks to my wife, Nancy), I pursued habits that fostered long-term happiness. The high achiever and workaholic entrepreneur was sobering up to what really matters in life.

Despite some health issues with my kids and me being diagnosed with cancer at fifty years old, this new curve has given me a robust coping mechanism. A happier person copes much better with life stress, a well-documented fact.

Being open to fun has always characterized my life. I add some vibe and swag to life, whether walking, working, doing chores, or teaching. Life does not have to be dull!

Africans have always had fun in our value system, and modernization has begun to steal that from us. Look at how the black American community has added zest to not only America but the world. The pastors in Alabama, the hip-hop culture, the soul music, and even the walking-with-a-swag of former President Obama!

The world loves it, as shown by the uptake of black entertainment such as hip-hop, rap, R&B, and even break-dance, of which I was part of the wave in the 80s.

The San people of the Kgalagadi, the Asante people of Ghana, and the Zulus of South Africa still dance and sing as a vital part of their cultural inheritance. I can add that it's critical to their survival and thriving.

Right now, Nigerian music is taking the world by storm with its fun-loving essence and African drum beats. Even Gaël Monfils, a black French athlete, has amazed the world with his unorthodox and highly entertaining style of play at the highest levels of tennis.

Indeed, happiness is an inside job. We all strive for happiness, and I hope that through reading my example, you can get rid of the happiness-destroyers of your life and embrace

EntreHappiness, my concept for an entrepreneur who lives a happy and fulfilling life.

And like any other habit, you need to invest time and energy to transform into a happier person. A genuinely thriving and happy entrepreneur can be more productive and contribute more to society, and research on happiness supports this. According to happiness scientist Sonja Lyubomirsky, results from 250 meta-studies demonstrated that happier people:

- Make better leaders and negotiators
- Demonstrate better productivity, flexibility, and ingenuity
- Show better resilience to depression, trauma, and stress
- Live longer and have healthy social relations[1]

So, I trust you will agree with me that this is worth investing in for a better self, entrepreneur or not! The self-destructive habits of many entrepreneurs have to stop. This is the essence of this book: you can lead a pleasant life full of innovation and creativity.

The Gift of Now

I agree with Steven Pinker in *The Better Angels of Our Nature* that the world has become a better, less violent place with an abundance of food, energy, and technologies. Yes, Africa is still on catch-up mode, but accessibility has improved immensely.

The health revolution has kicked off, and this is exciting for us entrepreneurs who want to hang around and keep contributing to mankind. I have four granddaughters, and my desire to see them grow up heightened my focus on living a long, healthy life, a concept I have named happierspan. Not just a long life but a happy and vibrant one.

We are in the most technologically advanced society there has *ever* been. The world advances daily, and if we aren't taking advantage of it, it's going to advance right past us. We should be excited to use these developments as aids to our benefit. Technology is the best bet for Africa and the rest of the developing world to catch up.

Technologies such as AI, synthetic biology, solar, drones, and IoT are increasingly being democratized and demonetized. It is the best time for us to uplift our people from strife and poverty and close the gap with the developing world.

I also want to highlight how modernization values have hurt the very culture that is so much a part of our identity. With happiness, we can reclaim what makes us human. After we find happiness, we can focus on the unlimited possibilities that our unique society offers us.

It's possible to become a better you.

This is the story of how I unpacked the inner game of entrepreneurship—and how you can do the same.

PART ONE
THE GIFT OF ENDURANCE

CHAPTER ONE

BOTSWANA: AFRICA'S BEST KEPT SECRET

A nation without a past is a lost nation,
and a people without a past is a people without a soul.
—Sir Seretse Khama, First President of Botswana

Most of my story takes place in Botswana, a small, arid country nestled at the heart of Southern Africa. We're often mistaken to be part of the country South Africa, our much larger neighbor (nearly 65 million people compared to our 2.5 million) to the east and south, but we are our own nation, thriving and persevering in our own way.

To some extent, Botswana and I grew up together. I was born in 1969, three years after my homeland attained independence from England. During my childhood, I was living in the most exciting period of the country's development.

At the time of our independence, Botswana ranked among the world's poorest nations. Our rural population survived on subsistence agriculture with little opportunity to rise above, and the government budget was supported by England. There were no cities and few paved roads.

Then, everything changed.

The discovery of diamonds in Botswana boosted this relatively unknown country to become one of the fastest-developing nations in the world. De Beers, a powerhouse in the global diamond industry, partnered with the Botswana government and pushed our economy forward. By the 90s, we had reached upper-middle income due to the diamond industry.

Botswana is a success story in the developing world. Many other African countries succumbed to a "resource curse" when leaders profited themselves at the expense of the citizens when endowed with vast reserves of natural resources. In the 80s, we were surrounded by neighbors in conflict as Namibia and Zimbabwe fought for their independence, and black people fought against Apartheid in South Africa.

Amidst these conflicts, our new government had to navigate the challenges of pulling its population out of poverty. Before he was elected president, Sir Seretse Khama helped gain independence from Britain. With his expertise, he then led the country to become an inspiring nation on the global stage.

My country's leadership underscored the humility of our people, as expressed by the Setswana proverb, "*Ntwa kgolo ke ya molomo,*" roughly translated to "The best way to deal with conflict is through dialogue."

Central to such principles was our Southern African core culture of "Ubuntu" ("*Botho*" in our Setswana language), which loosely translates to, "You are a person because of other people." This humility expressed by our leaders stemmed from this innate Ubuntu culture that promoted solidarity, compassion, humanness, communalism, and democratic governance through our Kgotla system. We'll talk more about Ubuntu in Chapter Seven.

Not only was Botswana one of the most successful economies in Africa, but it was also known for peace, security, and governance. Botswana provided sanctuary for leaders such as Nelson Mandela and Mozambique's Samora Machel, who were both involved in the liberation of their countries. We are a people of grace and warmth.

To put the icing on the cake, Botswana is home to one of the most beautiful areas on Earth, with its unique flora and fauna, which are found in the Okavango Delta and Chobe areas. These are home to an amazing diversity of wildlife that is still surviving in largely undisturbed natural spaces.

We have conservation rules for these areas, including anti-poaching and tourism guidelines. We are also home to the world's largest population of elephants, over 130,000, and the Big Five animals thrive in their natural ecosystems. As one of Africa's top podcasters and bloggers, Wode Maya recently posted after visiting, "Botswana is definitely Africa's hidden crown jewel."

Botswana's 2.5 million population is spread in an area the size of France (which has roughly 68 million people), making it a very sparsely populated country. Here, people live side by side with wildlife, huge Kgalagadi grass plains, and amazing open areas with some of the best sunset views in the world. I became an entrepreneur in a beautiful country with a vibrant, unique democracy and a development journey admired by the world. A truly best-kept secret!

Building a Nation

In order to understand the importance of my country, you first have to know how it came to be what it is today. Back in the 1800s, before we were under British control, the chiefs of the largest tribes in the area faced the threat of being conquered by the Boers (Dutch Settlers) of South Africa who had arrived in the 17th century in Africa and were in an expansionary mood, displacing African tribes along their way.

As a result of these worries, Sechele I, King of the Bakwena people of Botswana, defeated the Boers' attempted invasion with the assistance of other Kings of Bangwaketse and Bamangwato and the London Missionary Society (LMS) missionary David Livingstone. This is known as the Battle of Dimawe in 1852. Many believe that if our people had not been successful, we would currently be part of South Africa.

Although they were successful, they faced many losses, both in this battle and in the years that followed, and they knew they needed help to secure long-term victory. As a result, Sechele I and the two other leading Kings, Bathoen I of Bangwaketse and Khama III of Bangwato, sought protection from the English reign, and Botswana was declared a British Protectorate in 1895. Bechaunaland, as it was known, became a typical colony under the Queen of England.

Little happened during the time of the protectorate, and we were administered by the colonial administration, with the capital as Mafikeng. While surrounding areas changed with outside leadership, Bechaunaland remained calm and relatively peaceful.

The only major development was the railway line that passed through Botswana from South Africa to Zimbabwe. It was developed by the British imperialist Cecil John Rhodes, who had a dream for connecting the Cape to Cairo.

The men of Botswana, like other colonies, were roped into participating in the two world wars on the side of the Allies, and my grandfather Modiri Moiloa was assigned to North Africa in the first World War in 1917. So, our family has also contributed to world peace with thousands of other men from Southern African British colonies.

Cecil had been drawn to South Africa after the discovery of the richest diamond in the world in 1870 on a farm owned by the De Beers brothers. The mining company was named De Beers Consolidated Mines and is the same company that has partnered with the Botswana Government for the mining of the Botswana-rich deposits.

A few years after the diamond discoveries, gold was discovered in the Johannesburg area of South Africa, conforming to the rich natural resources of Africa that are still playing out today.

In 1925, a man named Seretse Khama became king at age four alongside his uncle, Tshekedi Khama, who was his regent. When he was older, Seretse studied in South Africa and then in England, where he met Ruth Williams, a white woman.

Their marriage sparked outrage from South Africa, whose apartheid beliefs legalized racism, and from some tribal leaders, who wanted him to marry one of his own people. The Apartheid philosophy of racism was introduced in 1948 when the National Party came into power and illegalized interracial marriages.

One of those opposed was his uncle, who demanded he annul his marriage and return to take his rightful place as Chief of Bangwato. When Seretse refused, Tshekedi Khama left the capital village, Serowe, with his supporters and founded a new village, Pilikwe. Meanwhile, Seretse returned to Botswana with his wife. Encouraged by a group of like-minded friends, he established the Botswana Democratic Party (BDP), which dominated the Botswana political landscape and continues to do so now.

Four years after the BDP was founded, Bechaunaland became the Republic of Botswana with Seretse as the first president. Before diamonds were discovered, the country, classified as one of the poorest in the world, was financially dependent on England, and agriculture was the main source of livelihood for the citizens. The discovery of diamonds completely changed our socio-economic outlook.

This is the environment I grew up in. You will learn more about my childhood in Botswana in Chapter Two.

Triumphs Beyond Borders

Since gaining independence, Botswana has made a mark on the world. The West often portrays African countries as caught up in poverty and conflict, but that is far from the whole story. We are full of entrepreneurial spirit, especially in the younger generations.

Botswana and many other African countries have made significant economic progress over the years. It is true that there are some countries still in troubling circumstances, but it is wrong to assume that is the case for the whole 1.2 billion African population.

The cultural landscape of Botswana was well-captured through Alexander McCall Smith's *The No. 1 Ladies' Detective Agency*. Smith lived in Botswana for a few years and sought to capture the lives and cultural norms of the people through this fiction series.

The book became a national bestseller and was turned into a series starring American actress and singer Jill Scott. The twenty-three books and the show did a great job of advertising the simple lives of African people living in a cultural and economic transition. It showed our desire to simply be happy amidst all the changes in our society.

For a country of 2.5 million, we also have many achievements on the global stage:

- **Miss Universe and Miss World:** In 1999, Botswana's first contestant in the Miss Universe pageant, Mpule Kwelagobe, won, a victory that showed that Africa is a place of beauty and grace. In 2024, Lesego Chombo was crowned Miss World Africa and made it to the top four of the Miss World competition.
- **Olympics:** In the 2020 Olympics, Isaac Makwala, Bayapo Ndori, Zibane Ngozi, and Baboloki Thebe won the bronze medal for Botswana in the men's 4x400m

relay, also setting an African record for the race. It was Botswana's second-ever medal at the Olympics, following the silver by Nijel Amos for the men's 800m in 2012.

In the 2024 Olympics, Letsile Tebogo ran the 200m and won our first-ever gold medal. He became the first African to win gold in the event and the youngest to win the event since 1956. He set an African record (19.46s), and he is now the fifth fastest man in the 200m. The men's 4x400m relay team, Letsile Tebogo, Busang Kebinatshipi, Bayapo Ndori, and Anthony Pesela, won silver.

• **Off-Road Motor Sport:** Off-road motorcycle sensation Ross Branch was crowned the 2024 W2RC FIM Champion. The victory made him the first African rider to win the World Championships, marking a historic moment for Botswana and for rally racing on the continent. Earlier in the year, he was second at the Dakar Rally 2024, again a first for Africa and Botswana.

These accomplishments showcase Botswana's potential on the world stage. We proved that we could succeed globally, and it brings me joy to imagine the young people who were inspired to strive for greatness. When one person shows it can be done, more will follow.

Our third president, Festus Mogae, became a public servant as an economist and later entered the political scene, serving as the Vice President and the Minister of Finance before becoming the president. During his time in office, he promoted diversification beyond diamonds, called for accountability in leadership, and maintained a stable government.

President Mogae's most significant effort was in combating the HIV/AIDS epidemic, which became an existential threat to the country, lowering life expectancy to below 60. He received recognition for this work, including the 2008 Ibrahim Prize for Achievement in African Leadership. Even after his presidency, he continued to advocate for HIV/AIDS treatment and protection globally. We need leaders who protect the well-being of the people, and I am proud of his international recognition.

While Botswana's global achievements are impressive, our hospitality has the biggest impact on guests from across the world. As an adult, I have interacted with hundreds of visitors who are deeply touched by the warmth of Batswana.

Botswana's hospitality is a testament to our warm culture and heritage.

We forge deep social connections, and we inherited a family-focused mindset from our forefathers. After my friend and the former VP at Yahoo, Salim Ismail, visited Botswana for a week in 2023, he told me, "Oabona, I have traveled to over 100 countries, and Botswana is still one of the few civilized countries that exist."

Salim and I paid a courtesy call to the Office of the President to meet His Excellency the President of the Republic of Botswana, Mokgweetsi Eric Keabetswe Masisi. He also went on a safari at the Okavango Delta, which is a UNESCO World Heritage Site. He was enthralled by the beauty and the natural state of the flora and fauna.

Salim visited the Jwaneng Mine, part of the Debswana Diamond Company, so he could appreciate the backbone of Botswana's economy. He was visibly impressed by the world-class operation and the talented team of engineers. He got to touch the unpolished diamonds that would later be shipped across the world.

People from other parts of the world are hungry to learn about unique cultures, traditions, successes, and experiences!

I tell my Toronto entrepreneur colleagues stories about chasing lions from our farm as they kill and eat our cattle, and I can see the sparkle in their eyes with awe and admiration of such experiences.

One of Botswana's impressive stories was how we got to build our first university in the early seventies. The president called upon the citizens to contribute a cow each for its construction. Thousands of citizens donated cows to make this idea a reality.

Livestock at the time was still the biggest sign of economic stability or progress in a family, and donating cows was a sign of a nation that was united and prepared to part with the little they had. Now, tens of thousands of graduates have gone through the University of Botswana to build the country, including me.

We as a country have a lot to offer the world as a whole. We are capable of great success, and our rich and vibrant culture is full of beauty and joy. Every day, we disprove the outdated stereotypes about Africa.

The Price of Progress

Later on in my life, I reflected on the happiness of my childhood compared to kids today. We were relatively happy despite the lack of resources and amenities that are available to today's generation.

Many of my friends think I romanticize this life of daily struggle, but at the time, we did not know anything different, so we had no better life to compare it to. Farming and working the earth were calming, and we had our tight families' support systems. Community values and relationships were important across the country and Africa as a whole.

Cultural experts Ronald Inglehart and Christian Welzel researched the nature of secularism and self-expression in cultures. A culture can either have strong ties to religion (traditional) or a secular approach (secular-rational). A country will also either focus on economic and physical security (survival) or equality and personal fulfillment (self-expression).

Inglehart and Welzel believe that as a country becomes more modern, it will shift toward secular-rational and self-expression. At this stage, people will focus more on personal choices instead of their basic needs. During Botswana's economic growth, we moved away from survival and traditional values, following this modernization trend.

In some ways, I'm nostalgic for the culture of our people when we were still in the traditional and survival state. I don't want to justify the poverty-stricken life we often had, but some of our developments altered the community values that were once a strong part of our culture. When economic development took priority, we ignored the psycho-social elements that led to a happier society.

Botswana has been a particularly special case as the cultural transition has been very fast, moving from survival (poor country) to a mix of traditional and self-expression values (upper middle-income status) in just a period of about 25 years. This has brought about a clash of cultures and some level of confusion in our population, leading to some social ills creeping into our once tight-knit communities.

The culture of individualism and "dog-eat-dog" is indicated by the rise in mental health challenges and increasing levels of corruption. In spite of her Christian faith, my mother resorted to what she grew up witnessing with her grandparents and relatives: the reliance on traditional medicines and ancestral anecdotal spirits. This culture clash was confusing for me at the time.

The biggest factor working to further the problem of our modernization is the increased corruption in recent years. Communities emigrated to Botswana in the 80s and 90s thanks to peace and lack of crime here. In the 2000s, political instability in Zimbabwe led to many people seeking refuge here. In collaboration with the United Nations High Commissioner for Refugees, our government provided food, shelter, and healthcare in refugee camps.

Now, inequality and the changes brought on by modernization have made the environment toxic for many of these communities. A culture that was once driven by community relationships and the joy of life is now driven by individualism and consumerism.

This concern preoccupies my mind as an entrepreneur and even more so as a man passionate about happiness. As the saying goes, we've thrown the baby out with the bathwater by developing our country at the expense of our souls. The modern values we adopt should lead us *toward* happiness, not away from it.

Despite Botswana and Africa's bad rankings on the UN's World Happiness Reports, it is within our control to change the trend and create better lives for our people.[2] We should be driven by soulful matters, not by material wealth. It's time to use our natural talents to live purposeful lives filled with passion and perseverance. We can endure these challenges and prove we are better than ever.

Even though we have seen rapid economic growth in Botswana, constraints on start-ups make it hard for entrepreneurs to develop their own businesses. Although the founding government leaders laid a strong foundation, the later leaders only maintained this system, doing nothing to raise Botswana to the next level.

According to the Science, Technology, and Innovation (STI) policy review by the United Nations, Botswana is below its expected level of innovation based on its income and compared to its peers in the upper-middle-income group.[3]

The most challenging hindrance to entrepreneurship is the lack of funding. I faced this and other challenges, including the well-entrenched bureaucracy, poor implementation of policies to modernize the country, and an inward-focused economy that doesn't attract foreign investors and talent.

Thanks to the endurance I learned, an endurance that exists in the very history of this country, I focused on my passion for helping the people of Botswana to grow and thrive. Like Frank Sinatra's song "My Way," "I faced it all, and I stood tall and did it my way."

I guided the teams at my consulting firm, Innolead, with positivity and a desire to make a difference in the companies we serve, which are primarily blue-chip organizations. Our brand became a household name in the market of innovative consulting.

Inspiring Future Change

In many ways, I have tried to use my influence to change certain aspects of my country. In 2002, I partnered with futurologist Clem Sunter. Sunter's strategic planning techniques help countries make long-term plans by identifying previous trends and developing future scenarios. We sought to convince the Botswana government to implement these techniques.

After several workshops with industry representatives and SNR government officials, I was told that despite interest in the work of the program, no department was able to take on the function. I hoped the then Botswana National Productivity Centre, who we had partnered with, would take on the challenge, but they didn't.

This kind of rejection was not new to me. Years before, I was a junior engineer for the Debswana mine, and I met Clem in South Africa, where he was an executive at Anglo American and a leader, speaker, and writer in Scenario

Planning. I suggested that the mine adopt the strategic planning concept and build a future planning office. Already, the mining company Anglo-American had a futuristic planning office along with other global companies like Shell Oil and ICL. But again, it was not to be, as the mine leadership did not approve.

Both of these situations were frustrating for me. I knew of a concept that could build an innovative culture, push bold decision-making, and move us to be a global leader. In short, I had an answer to bring us to the next level, but I was rejected.

The concept has been adequately proven in successful cases like how Shell Oil managed to not only survive the 1970s oil crisis but come out even stronger. Countries like the UAE use future scenarios to plan ahead and exploit emerging technologies faster than other nations. UAE has succeeded in diversifying its economy from over-reliance on oil to now oil contributing 15% of GDP.

UAE even went to the extent of appointing a Minister of the Future and a Minister of Happiness!

As you will see, I am very passionate about happiness. The book that most moved me was by the UPenn professor of positive psychology, Martin Seligman, *Authentic Happiness*. Marty, as he prefers to be called, is regarded as the father of Positive Psychology and has influenced countries and companies to build happiness into their structures.

I reached out to him a few years ago, and he expressed his keenness to support any initiative for Botswana on happiness. He was surprised that Botswana ranks so poorly on the UN annual happiness rankings.

Marty and his teams have slowly developed models to build resilience and happiness at a young age with schools. They started the Positive Education (PE) model in Australia in 2008, and ever since, it has been adopted in many countries such as Peru, Mexico, the USA, and the UAE.

Seligman's PE experts have demonstrated the correlation between student happiness and academic performance. This drove me to want to introduce this in Botswana, for which, through the assistance of Marty, we connected with the team that implemented the concept in Australia.

Positive Education has an amazing impact on teachers, uplifting their state of well-being. Students have benefited from reduced bullying, fewer mental health issues, kinder students, and improved grades. Who wouldn't want that for their children?

With this in mind, I attempted to introduce this to the Ministry of Education in Botswana, so we started working with kids to influence their future well-being in Botswana. We arranged a number of meetings with the principals of the Ministry of Education, and they were impressed by the positive education models and agreed that Botswana requested something like that.

However, the initiative came to a sudden end as they complained that the Ministry did not have any funds for such an initiative. They even requested that Innolead fund the initiative, after which we indicated that medium-size consulting firms were unable to.

All we wanted was for the Ministry to allow us to conduct a funded Proof of Concept (POC) at a few targeted schools that are underperforming. The cost was mainly to fund the Australian team as technical partners. Once again, the project failed before it started.

Fast forward to today, the education performance in Botswana continues to deteriorate with most secondary schools having pass rates well below 50%. A country with such a low population should not be allowing young kids to go to waste, with some ending up as unskilled, poorly paid workers in farms across the country. I again approached the Ministry to plead for positive education intervention.

As I write this book, I decided with other concerned stakeholders and education experts in the country to arrange a national Education Pitso (conference) where a resolution will be presented to the government to stop the bleeding in the education system that was once the pride of Africa. I am one of the beneficiaries of the earlier success of the systems where teachers and students were motivated to perform.

This is the story of our systems in Africa. It is a challenging environment to innovate and introduce new ideas and technologies to uplift our people. But we have a duty to push for our ideas until someone realizes their importance.

Botswana, My Home Base

With all of my plans and ideas for a stronger economy, the question remains: Do I emigrate to a country that will give me a better reception?

I love Botswana, and I am passionate about doing everything I can to help us grow. This country is my base, the place out of which all my business flows. From the dusty streets of the village where I was born to our beautiful capital city, Gaborone, this is my home and always will be.

When one greets another in our Setswana language, we say, "*Dumela*," which translates to "agreeable" or simply "acknowledging another." This is a sign of the humanity that lives amongst us. You do not pass another person without acknowledging them. And that is why in our tradition, however many people you come across, you say, "*Dumela.*"

This is why I believe that other countries can benefit from our ideas. That is why I want Innolead to impact more countries, starting with broader Africa and expanding globally.

We have proof that it is possible. In 2001, China's middle-income population was just 3%. By 2018, that rose to

50% and keeps climbing. In two decades, hundreds of millions of people were taken out of poverty because of strong economic reforms. India has another fast-growing economy that is projected to join the large global economies by 2050.

Both of these countries have over 1.4 billion people, just bigger than the population of all of Africa at 1.2 billion. Imagine the impact we could have by leveraging our population as a continent!

If we follow their lead and unite as one African nation, we can pull our people out of poverty. We already have the African Continental Free Trade Agreement that allows for the free trade of goods and services across the continent. This is the first crucial step that can contribute to a prosperous Africa.

One of the problems with our innovation is that even if programs are implemented, once that initial excitement wears off, little is done to promote the longevity of the program. Fatigue and costs create struggles for entrepreneurs and dampen their spirits. We need to maintain cash flow and encourage frugality.

But there is hope.

One hot debate in Botswana was whether Debswana could diversify from diamonds. This precious resource is finite, but our economy continues to rely on it. Leading from the front, I arranged with my Debswana colleagues to engage government officials to explore the idea.

I wanted to bring in the ideas for future-centered planning in the scenario of a diamond market collapse. We even brought in Salim Ismail, who excitedly spoke with the president and other national leaders.

Unlike the previous times I tried to inspire change, the mine chose to seek a solution to this problem. Since 2023, we have been working together to plan for future investments outside of diamonds. After many years, I was finally successful in getting my strategy heard.

The more entrepreneurs we encourage to assist in governmental decision-making, the more we will be able to transform our people into a high-status developed economy. This is exactly what happened with South Korea, which, by 1943, had a much lower economy than Ghana. As time went on, Ghana remained steady, but South Korea maintained a growth mindset that pushed them ahead.

Countries around the world have demonstrated that it is possible to move their people from poverty to prosperity, and I am proud that Botswana is one of them. The next step is to unite Africa and share these strategies for the benefit of all Africans who see no way out of their struggles.

With our community-driven mindset, we can lead countries from surviving to thriving.

Chapter Takeaways:

- Botswana and Africa are at a crossroads regarding meeting the material requirements of our people and capturing the key essence of our heritage that builds happy lives.

- A strong political leadership that looks after the needs of its citizens is central to building a prosperous society.

- You can change your mindset to see challenges as opportunities for success.

- You can thrive despite the challenging landscape you grew up in, whether it be in Africa or across the world. Entrepreneurs like you can accelerate economic growth.

CHAPTER TWO

FROM SIMPLE BEGINNINGS TO SUCCESSFUL BUSINESSES

If you want to know the end, look at the beginning.
—African Proverb

I was a young boy growing up in Botswana long before I was an entrepreneur. I cared for my grandparents' cattle and played with my friends in the dusty streets of Gaborone. I never would have imagined myself advising other entrepreneurs, let alone being one myself.

I was born in 1969 to Andrew Ntutu Kgengwenyane and Eva Makholo Moiloa a year after they were married. In Botswana, we find a sense of belonging in our ancestry. My father was born into a prominent farming family, and my mother comes from the chieftainship of the Bahurutshe in South Africa.

I am married to Nancy Kgengwenyane, who comes from the Kalanga tribe in the North East of Botswana from a village called Changate. We are blessed with four children: Tshepo, Refilwe, Motheo, and Mbako.

Nancy has been an immense support to my entrepreneurial journey in many ways, and the children (and four grandchildren: Nakani, Anjela-Joy, Cloe, and Misha) have been sources of joy and purposeful living. Our adult children have lovely life partners in Erin Rivers for Tshepo and

Mompati Miller for Refilwe, living in Ottawa and Gaborone respectively. We are truly blessed.

It is common practice in African cultures to name a child after some other grown-up member of the family, and I was named after my mother's uncle, Michael Mmiga Moiloa. Through this tribute, I was called to be like him, a hard-working man who served others and honored his family. This was the mindset I grew up in, the need to reach my full potential, maintain my heritage, and make my family proud.

Whenever I walk around my mum's village of Dinokana, Mmiga's many sons and daughters would call me dad as a symbol of representing their father, who long passed away in 1963. An honor they expect me to live by as a respected elder in the village of royal blood.

Mmiga would never have the chance of becoming a chief of the Bahurutshe as, according to records, his mother was the seventh out of seven wives to their grandfather. In our culture, the one who rules is the son of the first wife, and being seventh meant very little chance!

While my parents were getting a divorce, my sister and I were put into the custody of my paternal family at Barolong Farms, a village in the southeast of Botswana. My life was very different than it is now.

I remember that every time a car passed by the nearby road with a white person, we would shout, "Lekgowa! Lekgowa!" which means "White man! White man!" Then, we would run after the car because we believed that white people would bring us sweets!

We were not exposed to other races and were always amused to see one. There were some white farmers who had settled in the area, but we hardly got to see them as they were very few.

When I think back on growing up in the village, I remember very well the close community connections and the calm routines of daily life. We relied heavily on the produce from crop fields and the livestock my grandfather Ramotuba owned.

The seasons were well balanced between the rainy summer season when we would plant the crops, and the winter season when we would harvest maize, sunflower, cowpeas, and groundnuts. During summer, we feasted on corn, watermelons, sweet reeds, and milk.

Without radio or television, our free time was spent playing, amusing ourselves with whatever we found. In our compound, we had several huts occupied by aunts and daughters-in-law. My sister and I would play and attend chores with our many cousins.

Every holiday, it was a tradition in Botswana for everyone to go back to their extended family in the villages. Bustling towns back in the day would be empty as everyone headed out to villages across the country. This meant holidays were full of even more kids our age to play with and family to spend time with.

It wasn't all play, though. We young boys were occupied with herding the cattle, sheep, and goats while the men were busy in the fields attending the crops. We have a saying that loosely translates to, "No boy should be hit by the sun in his blanket."

We woke up early, put a pot of porridge by the open fire, and then went out to help milk the cows. We selected the cows, made sure they didn't bother the man who milked them, and then carried the milk back to the homestead.

In the early hours of the morning, we prepared tea for the adults. We would even take our grandfather warm water for him to rinse his mouth as he sat up in bed. The cattle would be out grazing as early as 6 a.m. so they could be milked at around 10. At 11, we ate our meal of porridge and milk, and then we took the cattle back out to graze.

If we were lucky, we would kill a hare with our hunting dogs for dinner while we were out herding livestock.

Otherwise, we didn't often eat meat. Porridge and milk was a common meal for children.

In the evenings, we sat around the fire, telling stories and enjoying time together. Often, these stories would be lessons for the children, like tales of monsters to prevent us from going out after dark. Then, we would go to bed so we could do it all again the next day.

Without radios, television, and social media, we went to sleep early, averaging nine hours or so, and making it easy to wake up early again for morning chores. It was hard work, but we had fun together with these routines.

My Grandfather's Influence

Because my father was mostly absent, my grandfather was the primary male role model in my life, although it was a very short window of time when I got to live with them. I observed him a lot, paying attention to how he acted, his habits, and what he valued.

We also lived with his fiery wife, my grandmother, who we kids were scared of! She was very much the disciplinarian who would chase us to go play or whip us when we were naughty. We never knew what mood she was in! There was a special tree we hated because she would get all her sticks for whipping us from it!

My grandfather was a calm old man. Although he was illiterate, he was an entrepreneur and a very successful farmer. He had almost 200 cattle in addition to his fields of crops. In a society where cattle are the biggest commodity, the grand size of his livestock marked his success.

He also had a good heart and would often give to those in need, including lending out his tractors. On occasion, he would have his neighbors help slaughter a cow and then give them a share of the pieces (called *dirwe*) afterward. We would also have a pot cooking just for people who may pass by. Giving was a strong part of his nature and a quality that I try to reflect in my adulthood. We had a true life of strong, healthy relationships and close-knit communities.

As an entrepreneur, my grandfather had to deal with many challenges that threatened the success of his farm. Botswana is an arid country with unreliable rainfall patterns, and we would often get hit by droughts that led to country-wide crop failures and the death of livestock.

Despite this, he remained resilient and successful. Barolong Farms, our village, was regarded as the grain basket of Botswana at the time. I got part of the inspiration to succeed and work hard from this old, wise man.

My grandfather was born in 1899 and died at the age of 81 due to blood pressure complications. My grandmother outlived him by over 10 years, living until she was 91. These are the people who did lots of physical work and lived on mainly organic foods (sorghum meals, beans, milk straight from cows and goats, and free-range meats like goat, sheep, beef, and chicken).

In today's society with modernization, education issues, and an abundance of ultra-processed foods, the Botswana life expectancy is 61 years.[4] Clearly, something has changed.

Before meditating was even a common practice, my grandfather would spend hours sitting by a tree. He would even ask for a bucket of warm water for his feet, just like you can now find at spas. He was, in many ways, a man ahead of his time.

My grandfather could be a very kind and gentle man, but he was also just. Disciplining boys who go astray was still part of the culture. I remember one time when the senior herd boy, Tsimako, lost some of the family cattle after coming from *madiso* (grazing fields).

Since cattle were a great symbol of not only wealth but also prestige in the community, a boy losing them had to face the consequences. One of the men in the community was called to assist with a hearing process.

I was particularly concerned as Tsimako was like an elder brother, and he did most of the farm chores that required an older boy. The hearing happened at about dusk, and I went off-site to watch it. I could not clearly hear what was said, but in the end, Tsimako had to take off his shirt, lie down on the floor, and be whipped by the visiting man assigned to the task.

Because cattle ownership was so important, whipping was the common punishment for such a crime. It was distressing for me to observe such an event because I was relatively young, around eight years old. But that was the norm of the times!

A Herd Boy's Close Encounters

Some of my most vivid childhood memories are the ones full of mischief or peril. The details of these stories are clear in my mind despite the years that have passed.

Lost in the Bush: There was an older man who would normally herd the cattle, and one day, he wasn't there. Grazing was an all-day activity, so my grandfather could not do it alone.

On this day, I was out with the livestock by myself when suddenly, a storm came. The animals started to run in the direction the wind came from. I tried to keep up with them, but the more they ran, the stronger the wind got.

I was frantically chasing after them, trying to whistle and shouting for them to come back. Heavy rain and lightning surrounded me as I watched the animals scatter until they were all gone.

Losing the cattle is the scariest thing I could do because of how big of an offense it was in my culture. I was not

INNOLEAD

looking forward to telling my family what happened, but I knew there was no way I could get them back in this weather.

As I was walking home, I crossed a road I thought I had already passed, and I realized I was lost. Not sure where I was going, I just kept walking and turning different ways, hoping to find something that seemed familiar.

During those times, dangerous men would kidnap boys, put them in sacks, and use their body parts for traditional medicine. I kept alert to any noise or movement, terrified I would run into one of these men. It was mid-afternoon when I started off, and at about 5 p.m., I saw smoke on a homestead nearby.

I walked into the yard to find a family sitting around a fire. They were very welcoming to me and even brought me on horseback back to my home. My family was all very kind to the man who brought me back, but once he was gone, so were the pleasantries. They weren't happy that I lost the cattle.

Surprisingly, my grandfather graciously let me stay at home to dry off and warm up while they went looking for the livestock. I was lucky to not be punished, and it was a relief to be safe at home after being lost. I think my encounter of being lost and rescued derived sympathy from my grandfather.

The Black Mamba: Another major childhood memory is the time I was almost bitten by a black mamba snake. When I was younger, my mom got me a new bike. I can still picture it: a little red one with two supporting legs in the bike, like training wheels. Tsimako taught me how to ride. I specifically remember one time when he pushed me, and I ended up in a thorn bush!

When I was around eight or nine, I went out riding to my uncle's place about six kilometers away, sent by my grandmother to borrow some house needs. There was an eerie silence in the bush, and I was a little scared because of the

~ 26 ~

men who kidnap boys. When I turned at a fork in the road, I noticed something moving in the moretlwa (Velvet Raisin) bush nearby. I looked just in time to see a black mamba snake jumping at me as it hit the crossbar of my bike with a *bing*.

I screamed so loudly that my uncle and family heard me from their homestead nearby as I was a hundred meters from arriving. The mighty mamba rose above ground, looked at me (as if saying "I almost got you") and then disappeared into the bush.

Unable to ride the bike as I was shaking, I walked holding the bike to my side until I arrived. As soon as I got there, my uncle checked to make sure I was okay and was relieved to find I was not injured. If the snake had aimed just a little bit differently, I would not be here today as mamba poison is one of the most potent and can kill an adult within ten minutes.

You may not have lost your family's cattle or had a near-miss with a black mamba snake, but like me, your childhood adventures taught you valuable lessons. You likely have your own versions of my stories.

Was there a time when your family was frightened because you were almost hurt? Did you ever get lost or separated from your family, if only for a moment at the grocery store?

Even if you've never stepped foot in an African village, you likely have memories of your family gathering together during the holidays.

Playing outside, riding a bike, interacting with siblings or cousins, and helping with chores around the house, these unite us across the world. Even the idea that families share meals together and tell scary stories around the fire transcends cultures.

These childhood experiences help build endurance in us that will last our entire lives. Having to find our way back home or handling the monotony of chores can teach us what it looks like to withstand challenges.

Even as people are spread across the world, coming from different and unique backgrounds, we can relate to each other in that our past has led to our present and will continue to lead to our future.

Turning Tears to Knowledge

My mother, Eva Makholo Moiloa, otherwise known as Mma Mmiga, was born to Nkomeng and Modiri Moiloa in the village of Dinokana in South Africa, a village just 25 km from the Botswana border. Nkomeng was from Botswana out of a tribe called Bakgatla, with their capital being the village of Mochudi.

Like Modiri, my grandmother was from royal blood in Mochudi, and her maiden surname was Pilane. It was a common practice in those days for children of royal blood to marry into other royal families.

My grandparents (Nkomeng and Modiri) met whilst studying at Lovedale College in the Eastern Cape in South Africa, one of the few missionary colleges reserved for black people at the time in South Africa. Many black intellectuals had studied there, including former president of South African Thabo Mbeki and anti-Apartheid activist Steve Biko. Seretse Khama's uncle Tshekedi also went to Lovedale.

My father had relatives in Dinokana, and they used to ride bicycles from Barolong Farms to fetch oranges, which were abundant there with natural water springs and fertile soils. It was during one of those visits that my father met my mother and later asked her for a hand in marriage in 1968.

Interestingly, during the traditional wedding process, my father's cousin, Rre Mmono (representing my father's uncles), met my mother's older sister, Victoria Kelebogile

Moiloa. Soon after this first visit, my father and his cousin took the same trip again, this time to ask for Victoria to marry Rre Mmono.

So, sisters married cousins. My aunt Kelebogile and Rre Mmono later became key parts of our lives in Gaborone, and they were always supportive of my mother, Mma Mmiga.

My mother didn't know about my father's alcoholism until he showed up to their wedding drunk and barely able to stay on his feet. She had to navigate a painful marriage as a new bride in a new country. Her mother-in-law, my fierce grandmother, was harsh with her, and she missed her family back home.

When I was still young, my parents moved to Selebi-Phikwe, where my father worked as an administrative clerk for the BCL mine, and my mother was a primary school teacher at Tebogo Primary School. I was born a year after my parents were married, with my sister Boitumelo following me a year and a half later. Our brother Tshepiso was born five years later, and the lastborn, Lorato, nine years after.

Although my sister and I have a small age gap, she has always looked up to me as the older sibling. My siblings call me, "Buti," short for *aubuti*, meaning older brother. In this way, I had to step into the role of the eldest, especially after my parents divorced. I wore this heavy responsibility proudly, and I think this contributed to my early maturity and leadership roles at an early age.

Memories of My Father

I have very few happy childhood memories of my father. Before I even knew the term abuse, I became used to the sounds of a belt thrashing and my mother's screams. Some nights, we could hear them arguing, and my mother would leave to seek shelter with our neighbors. But no matter what she went through, she always came back to take care of her children.

One day, my sister and I were playing hide and seek with our friends on the street. My father came home earlier than usual, and when he saw us covered in dust and dirt, he was furious. He forced us under the shower, the cold water slamming against us on full blast. We cried and banged on the door to be let out, but he kept it firmly closed to our shock.

It felt like we were there for hours, the cold water stinging our skin as we struggled to comprehend why our own father could be so mean. When he finally turned off the water, we hurried away, but the damage was already done.

To this day, I sometimes lose my breath when I shower or go swimming.

One Saturday afternoon, my father took me to a soccer game to watch the local team, the Copper Chiefs. I was excited to spend time with him, but instead, I spent the whole time alone as my father sat with his friends drinking away as they enjoyed the match.

Another time, my father took me along to a store in the mining town to buy some groceries (I assumed!). But to my bewilderment, right in front of me, he picked up some chili spices, put them in his pockets, and walked right out of the store without paying! It was a shocking experience for a seven-year-old me, and I lost a lot of respect for him because of his blatant disregard for the law.

At the same time, he was still my father, and I craved quality time with him. I saw how he hurt my mother, my siblings, and me, but I could not shake the desire that he would love me as his son.

It was only later in life, when he was in his sixties, that my mother forgave him, and she graciously encouraged us to also reconcile with our father. She was wise enough to understand that reconciling with our father would be good for our well-being in addition to hers. The Christian in her was calling for forgiveness and reconciliation.

Many people told me he was very bright, and I was finally able to see that side of him. He was no longer an alcoholic. In fact, he had two strokes that almost killed him because of his drinking, leading him to hate alcohol and smoking.

It was awkward for a few years, but we managed to build a warm relationship with him until his passing at seventy-seven years old. In the end, it was a happy ending in a positive light with our father, who had also become a Christian.

On reflection, I have become a typical "single mother" boy with my siblings and, worse still, with abuse having characterized our childhood upbringing. Enrolling in therapy was helpful in understanding the negative impacts of childhood trauma and building guardrails to still become a productive and thriving member of society.

Such trauma was bound to impact our relationships and how we relate to people in general, whether in the workplace or to friends and family. My deliberate intentions to invest in happiness and well-being principles have been important in this regard, and although we can still be haunted by elements of the dark past, we need not become victims.

I refuse to become a prisoner of my dark past and will do all to live a "good life" of virtue as articulated by ancient philosophers like Aristotle.

Resilience Through Hardship

In 1977, my mother filed for divorce when the marriage became intolerable. It was a hard decision to become a single mother to three kids. We had to move out of the house the mine provided for my father, and we relocated to Gaborone after the divorce. We were so happy to be with Mum again after living with our grandparents.

Life was not easy for our family, especially for my mother. She spent her days helping us with our homework, cooking, and pursuing her own further education, often studying late into the night. When she enrolled in a program to study for a diploma in Education for two years at the University of Botswana, her income was halved, making it challenging for her to make ends meet.

We survived on simple meals like *motogo*, a soft porridge made out of sorghum. We looked forward to Sundays when she prepared the best meals, including chicken and rice! Meat was a treat we only got on occasion.

We had no electricity in our house at that time, so Mum bought firewood we would chop together to fit onto our charcoal stove. At night, the house was lit with candles and paraffin lamps.

She was so frugal she would not buy herself new dresses for a long time so we kids could look like other kids and always have food on the table. She would also share with me how, unfortunately, she was not receiving any maintenance support from our father as per the divorce conditions, which made it even more challenging for her.

Once my mother successfully completed her diploma in Primary Education, she was promoted to Deputy Head Teacher at Lesetlhana Primary School in Ramotswa, a village just outside Gaborone city. Before then, she taught at Camp Primary School in Gaborone.

A few years later, she was promoted to Regional Education Officer, overseeing a number of schools in the Southern part of the country. She eventually became Principal Education Officer in the Ministry of Education based in headquarters in Gaborone, now driving primary education policies for the country. Her students and fellow teachers loved her, and many of her students went on to be very successful captains of industries.

Even though she taught at a different school from where we went, she would assist us with our homework and even give us extra work, to our dismay! Excelling academically was an imperative for her kids, and it did deliver as all four of us went through university.

This drive for education was prevalent in every aspect of her life.

Mma Mmiga, as my mum is fondly called, was very close to her elder sister, Victoria (Mma Mmono). Our aunt was the longest-serving headmistress of Lesedi Primary School in Gaborone (where we went for our primary school after arriving from the village), one of the best-performing government schools in the country at the time.

These two phenomenal South African-born women made a mark in their new country despite the challenges of their Bantu Education, which legalized segregation in schools and led to low-quality education for black South Africans.

Mma Mmiga was a truly resilient woman who did not succumb to the challenges of life thrown at her. Today, my wife Nancy and I are raising four kids, which still isn't easy for a two-parent family. Mma Mmiga not only persevered in the midst of sometimes life-threatening challenges, but she thrived.

I still have beautiful memories of our Christmas holidays with her in her home village of Dinokana, where she would be with her siblings, all happy while reconnecting with them.

Celebrations like when she graduated from university were momentous for her. She encouraged us to participate in school activities, and as siblings, we participated in the Boy Scouts and my sister in the Girl Guide movement. These contributed to building character but were also enjoyable as we mingled with other kids in fun activities like camping.

But, what appeared to really support her was her ever healthy social connections with family, friends, and work colleagues. She was very close to her teacher colleagues, and she would visit them over weekends in the old-fashioned way of a cup of tea and chatting under a tree.

I learned a lot from her, and the best gift I could give her was to complete my education to university level and become financially independent and contribute to my society. Her calling as a teacher, toiling even over weekends to ensure her students passed, was particularly touching.

My Mother, the Visionary

As the firstborn, I always had a close relationship with my mum, and she relied on me to help take care of the family. I would go with her to visit her sister and other relatives so I could play with the other children. Some of my most valuable friendships were forged there while my mother chatted with her friends.

When there weren't kids to play with, I listened to the adults discuss social issues or current events, learning from their wisdom and developing my own opinions. My maturity blossomed during these afternoons.

Despite all the challenges in her life, my mother was always very warm. She was simultaneously kind and challenging, and she embodied a driven mindset with very strong leadership skills.

I remember one day when I got home after curfew playing street soccer with friends, my mother was angry with me for coming home late, so she told me to pick out a stick she would use to punish me. Hoping she would take pity on me, I picked out a large, thick stick, but she used it on me anyway.

I certainly learned my lesson!

She always made sure we understood the importance of our choices and how they can affect not only ourselves but other people. Not punishing me would have shown me

I could get away with disobedience. It instilled in me the motivation to do what was right and think about the consequences of my actions.

My mother was very open with us about her goals and desires for education and all she hoped to achieve. She was the first visionary in our family, showing us what it looked like to pursue our dreams and prioritize the people in our lives.

She had unmatched resilience and grit, two qualities I grew to admire and continue to strive for to this day. Through her endurance in the face of single mother struggles, she showed that trauma does not have to turn to pity. Her unwavering moral code also kept her upright and embedded that in us. Even her former students would mention how "good manners" was number one to her even before academic performance.

Despite her disciplinarian behavior, my mother was loving, and we had a very close relationship. Regrettably, parental aloofness meant sometimes I was never entirely free to share my deeper issues with her. I now understand she was a woman of her time, operating in the context of her own upbringing.

Her passing in 2022 was a low moment for my siblings and me. We, however, found solace in that she had delivered her calling as an educator, mother, aunt, friend, and grandmother. She lived a rich life and impacted many.

As actor Denzel Washington once put it when mourning his mother's passing, "A mother is her son's first true love." I still have many positive memories of her that encourage me to keep going in doing good to society. She planted the seed.

Turning Tears to Knowledge

You are going to encounter stumbling blocks along your entrepreneurial journey, both professionally and personally.

You likely can recognize some you've already faced. I learned early on I could not let my circumstances define me or my story.

Throughout my life, I will continue to remember the painful experiences my father put me through. The images are clear in my mind decades later. Despite this, I move forward, recognizing no matter how difficult these barriers are, they can help me reach my full potential. Because I learned to adapt to these challenges when I was younger, I found it easier to do so as an adult.

I'm lucky I had my mother as an example of perseverance and strength. I encourage you to find someone like that in your life. Even if you aren't aware of it, people around you have kept going in the face of unimaginable pain.

Find those people and pick out the qualities you most respect. If possible, sit down with them and talk about their journey. Always be asking yourself: what is it about these people that make them so resilient, and how can I reflect that, too?

If I viewed my single income home and abusive father as permanent obstacles, I would not be where I am now. I believe it's impossible to ignore the troubles in your life. They will confront you whether you want them to or not, and if you're not prepared, they will cause more stress than you deserve.

My siblings and I are classic children from a "family break-up" structure. Our parents divorced when we were very young. I was eight years old, my sister Boi was seven years, and my brother Tshepi was only two.

One study has shown that if parents split up, a child will roughly be twice as likely to become a depressed adult as compared to children whose parents stayed together. It did not matter how old the child was when the separation occurred.[5]

To add salt to wound, another study concluded that, "As adults, people from single-parent families are more likely to die young and to get divorced themselves." We were on the wrong side of the statistics![6]

But my life has turned out the opposite as Mma Mmiga managed to set the foundation for hard-working and gritty kids who are thriving in spite of the mental challenges they faced at a young age.

My mother showed me to take control of the challenges I face in my life. Through how she modeled endurance, I realized she was not giving power to the problems she faced. Instead, she was taking that power back into her own hands. She took the tears life gave her and turned them into the knowledge she needed to thrive.

She taught me many key lessons that have shaped who I am today.

Overcome Obstacles: Mma Mmiga did not let trials beat her down. She showed us to let our tribulations build us up stronger than ever before.

Values and Moral Code: Your morals should direct your life. Turning against your values is like abusing your own propriety.

Healthy Relationships: Support structures are critical to building resilience. Mum was very close to her siblings, her extended family, her teacher friends, and her church community.

Curiosity: My mum introduced me to the free Botswana Daily Newspaper that she brought home every day. I would read it and listen to the news with her. This planted the seeds of my curiosity. She recommended books she learned about in her developmental psychology classes, which influenced my current pleasure in reading philosophy, psychology, and technology.

Happiness: Mma Mmiga showed us what it looked like to live a happy life. It was by no means easy, but she faced the world with optimism and joy. She found comfort in her community, invested in her children, drew pleasure from her work, and overall lived a celebratory life.

I will always carry these lessons with me. She showed me firsthand what endurance truly looks like. She bounced back better than ever before.

Remember, the trials you are facing right now may seem like they will last forever, but as the African proverb says, "However long the night, the dawn will break."

Chapter Takeaways:

- A calm and happy childhood full of hard work lays a solid foundation.
- Be inspired by role models who embody a life of endurance and resilience. Reflect on your parents' well-meaning teachings and actions. That could be what will drive your success.
- Everyone goes through challenges that alter their futures. Acknowledge the difficulty of trauma without letting yourself be overwhelmed by it. Spirituality and staying happy build resilience. Never hesitate to seek therapy support.
- Stand tall with your identity and be a proud member of the community and of Africa (or your continent). The confidence serves your right in negotiations and building businesses.

CHAPTER THREE

FROM SALARY TO STARTUP: MY ENTREPRENEURIAL JOURNEY

Every next level of your life will demand a different you.
—Leonardo DiCaprio

I grew up knowing little about entrepreneurship.

The path to success was not found in designing your own business but in climbing the corporate ladder. Achieving high grades guaranteed a government scholarship to university, or even better, a company like Debswana would take over the scholarship for high-end careers like medicine or engineering. These two studies were only available internationally, so you were assured an overseas education, mainly in the UK or Canada, at the time.

After I secured a scholarship, my first overseas trip was to attend the University of Southampton in the UK in September 1990. I had the opportunity to see the world and be exposed to life far from home. I was determined to take advantage of it as much as possible.

I stayed for four years, finishing with a Master's of Engineering in 1994. I started my career as a mechanical engineer at Debswana Mining Company, based at the prestigious Jwaneng Mine, which ranks as the most profitable diamond mine in the world due to its high concentration of high-value diamonds.

The workers there proudly call it the "Prince of Mines." Combined with the other two mines Orapa and Lethakane, it makes up 70% of De Beers' production and contributes to around 33% of Botswana's GDP.[7] It was a privilege to work for the company that played such a critical role in the economy of Botswana.

But I was not to last long.

My career started well, and my diligent approach to work was recognized by mine management. I read widely and was ready to challenge management where appropriate. I recall the engineering manager at the time telling me, "The problem with you, Oabona, is that you are mature for your age." I did not read much into the statement, albeit appreciated the compliment.

I would freely make suggestions to management and lead my sections with a creative and curious mind. I experienced ideas and empowered my teams to make decisions, try new ideas, and learn from mistakes instead of playing the victim.

I studied the well-entrenched hierarchical culture of the mine, where the boss seemed to be always right. Fortunately, the De Beers Debswana operations were very strong with graduate development and training programs, and I devoured theories of leadership and management at any opportunity.

I did supervisory development courses earlier as a junior engineer and went on to Management Development at Stellenbosch University in South Africa. I was selected as part of the group of Anglo/De Beers engineers to do the High Potential Managers program with the INSEAD business school.

The whole exposure to management and leadership thinking laid the ground for a strong interest in knowledge and insights. I also studied other business leaders as examples of what to do or not to do as a leader.

I studied business leaders like Henry Mintzberg, who popularly criticized Jack Welch, former CEO of General

Electric. He argued against Welch's strategy for downsizing and cutting costs, saying that it was harmful in the long run. I also read *Built to Last* by Jim Collins and Peter Senge's work on systems thinking. I was inspired by how the oil company Shell was able to predict the 1973 oil crisis through scenario futuristic planning.

I applied the theories I learned with my team, experimenting to see what achieved the best results. I also tested these theories with the larger corporate performance. My love for people became evident the more I visited workers at the engineering workshop floors, canteens, and tea rooms and enjoyed it.

I was shocked that workers had different messes based on rank. This made my leadership role difficult because I believed in equality irrespective of rank, and I was determined to break these structures.

The then GM, Mr. Derrick Moore, took a liking to me due to my outspokenness on issues affecting the mine, and I think he was touched by my challenging him on the Debswana operations business model shortly after being employed by the mine.

When I was a section manager, he would occasionally call me to represent him at community assignments where he was meant to deliver speeches as a keynote speaker. I recall being a special guest on his behalf to give a speech in the village of Kang and later in Machaneng. It became part of my development as I got to appreciate being treated as a VIP with a little flower placed on my blazer and a seat at the center chair with other community leaders.

It was a privilege that I cherished as I was exposed to life at grassroots village levels once more. It ignited my memories of when I lived a simple life in my home village and when I spent twelve months doing national service in the village of Pilikwe. It was a clarion call that our people deserve better lives, and the seed was planted in me that one day.

I could play a more significant part to impact their lives positively.

Stress and Strategy: Lessons in People Management

There was never a dull moment in the mining operations. On my usual weekly walks to check on my teams, I would listen to the bellowing sounds of the 200-ton trucks as they drove up and down the 200m pit and the squeaky conveyor systems as they transported ore.

In the mid-afternoons, we were required to evacuate certain areas as the mining teams would be blasting in the pits to expose the ore. Amidst this, men would be at work making sure all machines were powered up. One wrong step could lead to a quick death or undesirable production stoppages.

All those shiny stones would be sent to high-end stores across the world to make a newly engaged couple rejoice. We made people happy, and I realized we were actually in the beauty industry! All this blasting, odd noises, and men at work were to make some couple smile. It made me happy, and I wanted my teams to be happy as well.

One night, I received an urgent call. There had been a breakdown that resulted in a hydraulic failure at the mines. My team and I had to spend the following day investigating, and all plant operations had to stop. At the time, every hour spent on operations was a million pula lost, so halting production was extremely costly.

My adrenaline kicked in, and I was overcome with anxiety. There was a lot of pressure on me to lead the team and resolve the matter quickly. I found serious problems with the hydraulic system. We spent all night diagnosing the problem and arguing about how to solve it. As the night progressed,

I had to ensure the team members were able to go home and rest while the rest of us continued working.

We finally cracked it in the early hours. It was a very proud moment for the team, and I congratulated them heartily afterward. I learned a valuable lesson that I could only have learned in action: the discipline of working as part of a team, problem-solving, and working under pressure.

Another time, I was the manager on standby over a weekend. We had a roster as engineers and managers on the mine, and it was my turn that weekend to attend to any matters that required a senior person to attend to. While relaxing on a Saturday night at 11 p.m., I got a call from the mine team.

I thought it was just a usual call to update me about an equipment breakdown and notify me in case it got out of hand. The report was, "We found the body of a dead man on the processing screen and had to shut down the production process."

I thought it was a dream and was in shock. I kept asking the foreman if he was ok and reporting accurate information. He insisted it was real. I had to get myself together and support the team, who were clearly in distress.

I first had to call the General Manager and also alert the Government Inspector of Mines, as per the legal safety reporting protocols. My drive to the mine was one of the strangest I ever had. I couldn't believe the report, and I was scared that it was in my section because then I could be liable by law if there was a safety breach.

I arrived at the process plant, all quiet and eerie as they had to shut down everything. When I got to the Main Treatment Plant (MTP), the team was waiting for me and immediately directed me to the dead man's body.

It was a gruesome sight that will ever stay with me. We learned later that it was a young man from town who had come to the mine to commit suicide. We were partly relieved that the investigation proved we were not at fault, but it was also a deeply disturbing incident for me. I was twenty-seven at the time, and it wasn't easy to be reminded how hazardous the mine was. Fortunately, safety was a priority at the Debswana mines, and fatalities were rare.

I also learned valuable lessons outside of work. I quickly saw how our village communities looked at leaders with such high regard and relied on them for poverty relief. There was plenty of poverty in the villages near the mine. I visited them on weekends as part of my keenness to meet people. It was a shock to see that level of poverty just a few miles from one of the hottest mining assets on the planet!

The exposure to lectures and other learning facilitators in Botswana and South Africa planted a seed in my mind. In recognition of my skills, I was appointed to be part of the Jwaneng Mine Strategy in 1996. I would be on the mine team that worked with the expert global consulting firm Johnson & Johnson.

This was one of the most memorable highlights of my five-year career at the mine.

The external consultant exposed us to consulting methods that I found thrilling. I took the work of transforming the mine very seriously as I now had a clear position on the challenges faced. At the top of the list were the bureaucratic culture, rigid processes, and dictatorial leadership styles that stifled creativity.

The external consulting team was impressed with my insights, which were all a result of the training the mine had taken me through. As a result, I was appointed Chairman of the Change Champions Committee, which was charged with driving change across the different mine departments, and on occasion, we would take on the executive team.

The committee included even more senior members than me, like then senior HR manager Mrs. Wilhemina Makwinja, who contributed to my development. She later became a member of Parliament and Assistant Minister to the Government of Botswana.

As a change committee, we never hesitated to take on the executive committee whenever they strayed from the agreed transformation agenda. I recall an incident when the executive team decided to go on a retreat to Victoria Falls and do the popular white water rafting.

The change committee went berserk at the idea as one of the mine strategy pillars was cost saving and one of the agreed values was consultation on any matters that impacted staff.

A few months earlier, the mine executives had decided to shut the clinic that was housed in the mine operations area so that workers could have easy access whenever they had health-related issues. It also meant improved productivity as staff did not have to take extended leaves to go to the hospital that was ten kilometers away.

Staff had loved the idea of a clinic in their area of work as the mines are generally hazardous, and it's common for staff to have minor injuries. The executive team decided to shut down the clinic to cut costs, not even caring to consult staff as per our agreed mine values.

Now, the white water rafting trip contradicted the core values, and the angry mine workers told the Change Committee that they never trusted management. They had wanted to believe the executives would follow through, even if they had a deep sense of cynicism from past letdowns.

The Change Committee was mad, too, and we wasted no time in confronting the executive team. As the Chairman, I did not mince my words regarding the betrayal and how they were perpetuating the cynicism and the divide between workers and management. We succeeded in stopping the executive team from going to Victoria Falls for white-water rafting!

Breaking Free From Corporate Chains

It was around this time that I tried implementing scenario planning with Clem Sunter, as I talked about in Chapter One. The need for Debswana's transformation was magnified.

I proposed that I be sponsored for an MBA at a reputable university, and I discovered that other high-potential juniors at Anglo and De Beers were sent to the UK for further leadership development. I, however, was quickly shot down and reminded that Debswana had no such policy. Although I did not benefit from it myself, I did learn that I paved the way for future employees to be sponsored for their MBA.

I was increasingly realizing that Debswana may not be for me after all. The company was reluctant to change, and I knew I could not make a difference on my own.

One book that really impacted my thinking was *Control Your Destiny or Someone Else Will* by Noel Tichy and Stratford Sherman. The title alone was enough to transform how I think. I knew that I did not want my life to be defined by bureaucracy. Life is too short, and I had education and valuable experience to go and carve my life elsewhere.

This was a serious consideration. I loved my team, my fellow engineers, and my managers. I learned so much in this role. I worked with some of the most brilliant engineers. It was a work community I cherished.

But in the end, I knew leaving would give me the best growth moving forward. My love of knowledge dictated my career. I found my passions were intrinsic, and I could not deny their desire to grow. I truly wanted to control my destiny.

As a result, I soon moved on to a company called Geoflux, which offered consulting services in geology, hydrogeology, and environmental services. I was there for several years, and I will talk more about my experiences in the coming chapters.

After I left there, I finally started my entrepreneurial project. I was influenced by insights from the management programs I had done at UCT and University of Stellenbosch. I also read widely on scenario planning and used some of the techniques to learn from the future and plan my business idea.

I used the writings of Henry Mintzberg to inspire me, including assessing my distinctive competencies and competitive advantages and evaluating my trends and patterns. I rejected bureaucracy, which I found stifling while working in corporate. The heavy hierarchy of the mines did not sit well with me, and I desired to be free.

As a project manager at the mines, I had a level of competency I could leverage in my new industry. The Innolead idea was conceptualized in 2001, and we are now in our 23rd year. But the game has just begun!

The start-up period was grueling and taxing on my family and me. I later learned that most start-ups fail, and I can see why. I was starting a company in a space that was dominated by foreign businesses (mainly South African).

Somehow, with hard work and perseverance, I was able to break into the industry. Some of my most memorable assignments included the Botswana Building Society strategy to transform into a commercial bank in 2002, the Debswana Diamond Company's 5-year plan in 2007, Barclays Bank (now ABSA), developing a PMO (Project Management Office) for BCL Copper Mine and many others.

Similarly, I have guided government and mining houses with billion-dollar projects in terms of mapping requirements for capital projects, risk assessments, scoping projects, and execution methods. I have spoken at conferences in Botswana, Uganda, and Zambia at PMI conferences and similar, on project management and leadership.

From Start-Up to Industry Leader

Between 2002 and 2015, Innolead graduated from a start-up to a full-fledged consulting firm with over 20 employees. We competed effectively with other successful businesses, especially in corporate strategy and project management.

We have had projects that really tested us, such as the BCL copper and nickel mine Smelter Shutdown, which, for the first time, was awarded to a local company. It was a 45-day shutdown project that needed to be delivered on time with a budget of $15 million. Delays to the project would mean the planned maintenance shutdown had failed, costing the mine sales.

The project was delivered successfully and even saved some millions of pula for the mine. It was a significant milestone for us as we continued to mature as a consulting firm with a solid track record.

But the growth of the company did not come easy. Growing pains tormented us. Some key team members did not perform to expectations, and I had the difficult task of negotiating their exit with them. These were team members I had been in the trenches with, so it was emotionally challenging to have these conversations.

I was still very involved with the projects, and I would come home exhausted. We were growing the company under my stewardship as the founder. Some team members also showed signs of fatigue.

One of my most trusted managers, the current Head of Operations Chilipi Mogasha, painfully told me he needed to take a break and go on sabbatical for six months. He is an engineer like me, and he particularly struggled with the people management aspect of his role. It was a time of our growth when I needed managers (with over thirty staff) to cover some aspects of the business while I focused on business development and growth paths.

This happened the same year that I received an invite to the Strategic Coach program in Canada. When I first decided to join in 2015, I did not expect to be hooked.

They confirmed some beliefs I previously harbored and even practiced without knowing how to name them. It was an absolute revelation to join such a program that can contribute to transforming the lives of entrepreneurs.

We share experiences in these workshops with fellow entrepreneurs across Canada, the USA, and Europe. Co-founder of Strategic Coach, Dan Sullivan, and the program have impacted many lives on how we see the world and how we can turn our adventure into not only material success but also happier and fulfilling lives. I call Dan an entrepreneurial philosopher.

Attending the program on a 90-day basis also meant developing connections with fellow entrepreneurs and addressing one of the ills of entrepreneurship: loneliness.

In between the workshops, we would contact each other and also call the Program Advisors, meaning there is always a shoulder to lean on when in need. Most of the entrepreneurs have written bestseller books and also started podcasts. In fact, the motivation for me to write a book and start a podcast was born from the Strategic Coach floors.

Innolead grew to become a dominant player as a locally "home-brewed" company with the largest employment numbers as a management consulting company. We became a brand that the nation became proud of due to our endurance and self-belief.

The farm enterprise also experienced growth as I managed to secure additional farm space to 10x our practice. The original 6x6 km farm we secured in 2008 proved to be unprofitable based on the possible stocking rate for the area.

We bid for newly advertised farms and were awarded a 9,200-hectare farm that made our total farming area 13,000 hectares. Now, we can grow and develop a profitable farm!

We have a total of 600 breeding stock across the two farms and have started stud breeding with the Limousin-type cattle.

As Steve Jobs said, "I'm always amazed how overnight successes take a helluva long time."

My energies have reignited, and we've embarked on Innolead 2.0, which is going to make a broader impact on our people in Africa. Our passion for being at the frontiers of the latest knowledge and technology will take a new pathway to improve the lives of our people. Our aim is to make a positive impact on our people through leveraging insights and exponential technologies.

It's a scary but exciting challenge!

Chapter Takeaways:

- Be your authentic self! If I had stayed at Debswana despite the clear misalignment, I would have been increasingly unhappy.

- Take advantage of extra training or resources. You never know when pursuing a new interest could lead you to a new career.

- Read and never stop learning. I read at least 15 minutes a day on various subjects that interest me.

- Nothing happens without courage! Once you have explored your passions, make the call and quit if need be. You deserve to live the life you want, one that uses your God-given talents.

CHAPTER FOUR

GROWING GRIT

Even the lion protects himself against flies.
—African Proverb

Honestly, I've never seen myself as a brilliant individual in most endeavors I have embarked on. From my student days and tennis career to basketball and dancing and ultimately as a manager and entrepreneur, I have seen talent before me, and I can say there's more to success than being good at something.

Botswana's top junior tennis player during my time was simply raw talent with his graceful movements and shots. But even with his talent, we could not overcome the Zimbabwean tennis team. The best our player could get was a few games. The Zim team, both the girls and the boys, were simply too much for us, and we knew why.

The Zimbabwe team had better facilities and more organization. They had improved access to professional coaches, and some of them even had tennis courts in their homes. Players from Zimbabwe have participated in Grand Slam tournaments like Wimbledon, so they were exposed to the international game.

Their top junior player was Byron Black, the son of a global professional player, and there were rumors that the boy had to make hundreds of serve practices before going to school. Byron went on to become a professional tennis player, as well as his siblings, Wayne and Cara.

The Zim players were very gritty. They worked hard and used their resources to their advantage. Byron had spent his life dedicated to the sport, and no matter how hard our best player practiced, he just couldn't keep up.

Grit is the combination of passion and perseverance. When someone is gritty, they are able to overcome obstacles to achieve their long-term goals. It means sticking with your ambitions, not just for the short term but for however long it takes. It takes stamina.

Angela Duckworth is a leading grit researcher. She first became well-known for her TEDx Talk "Grit: The Power of Passion and Perseverance" and later wrote a book of the same title.

In her TEDx Talk, she describes being a math teacher and realizing that the students with high IQs were not always the ones who did the best. She then researched what allowed people to succeed in various settings. The one factor she found was grit. "Grit is living life like it's a marathon, not a sprint," she said.

The best thing she says can encourage grit is a growth mindset, as researched by Dr. Carol Dweck at Stanford University. This means believing that the ability to learn is not fixed. In other words, failure is not permanent.

In her TEDx Talk, Dr. India White describes GRIT as "Great Resilience In Time." It is grown over an extended period of time when you remain dedicated to the task at hand despite challenges that come your way. Resilience is short-term, but grit is long-term.

In their book *10x is Easier than 2x*, Dan Sullivan and Dr. Benjamin Hardy tell the story of renowned artist Michaelangelo. As a teenager, he studied corpses so he could learn anatomy, even though this was a crime at the time. His dedication to his craft led him to create the David statue, one of the most recognizable statues in history.

Michelangelo showed incredible grit in his work. He researched his craft despite the dangers, and he dedicated years of his life to art. He didn't let obstacles get in the way of his incomparable contributions to the world.

Angela Duckworth taught me that talent is not enough and that effort and passion are the main drivers. This reminded me of how my life circumstances, such as my disciplined mother who lived her career with passion, influenced me.

When I show up and focus on my mission, I invest time to achieve my goals. During my days in a dance group, I would dance by the mirror after studying so I could perfect my moves. I used our house wall at home to practice tennis volleys (for which my mother would scream at me for soiling the white walls).

My academic achievements were thanks to late nights in study rooms and libraries. Every major success in my life has required grit, even if I didn't know what grit was.

If you look at the world's most successful or notable people, you will find no shortage of grit. Helen Keller, for example, was an American educator and author who was blind and deaf at nineteen months old. She lived in a dark, silent world where she did not even know words.

With the help of her patient teacher, she eventually was able to communicate by finger signals on her hand, reading braille, and lip reading by touching the lips and throat of the speaker. She used her difficult situation to aid other blind people and advocated for rights for disabled people.

Malala Yousafzai was fifteen years old when she was shot for protesting Taliban reign in Pakistan. She was shot in the head but survived and went on to be the youngest person to receive the Nobel Peace Prize at seventeen. She believed it was her basic human right to get an education, and she did not back down when she knew that death could be the result of fighting back.

Most of the people we look to as the most influential, successful, and groundbreaking people faced challenges in their lives. We may think the elite are only so successful *because* of their life circumstances, but many of them rise up *despite* them.

Grit is a trait anyone can have. It may not come easily, but when you feel something pushing against you, you can push back to reach your goals. No one else can achieve your dreams for you.

Let me be clear that grit can be harmful. I believe that I sometimes pushed too much, like when I did a four-day non-stop strategy facilitation for a client, sometimes going well into the night. After the fourth day, I felt unwell, and my brain seemed to freeze. I knew that I had pushed too hard to satisfy a client at the expense of my health. Be careful not to confuse grit with overachieving and unnecessary stress. Quitting and starting afresh can also be a virtue.

Game, Set, Grit: The True Match Point

I played tennis during secondary school. Though equipment was expensive, my mum supported my interest and did what she could to make it happen. I joined the Botswana Junior Tennis Team, which was run by Mrs. Eupheumia Tlhaphane, referred to as the mother of tennis in Botswana because of her passion for junior tennis development and placing Botswana on the global map through the International Tennis Federation (ITF).

I started relatively late at thirteen and managed to catch up with my colleagues. I had the honor of representing Botswana as one of the top four players on the national junior team. We traveled to Zimbabwe and Zambia to compete.

I got to experience playing the sport at a higher level, and I was thrilled by the competition as well as the idea of testing myself to see how well I could do against other top players. I even got to ride in an airplane for the first time when we flew to Harare (then Salisbury) Zimbabwe, for tennis tournaments!

Although my tennis game was very much at an amateur level compared to global competitive standards, it was competitive in our world. We were thrilled to have access to professional coaches who grilled us on the game. The exposure to competitions regionally, especially the much higher standards in Zimbabwe, was essential for the growth of our skills.

The sport built character in me. It required strategy and an in-depth knowledge of the rules. Whether I won or lost, I needed to approach it with humility, never being prideful or complaining. A loss did not make me a bad player, and a win did not make me better than everyone else. I was schooled on good habits of competition, thanks to coaches who included a visiting professional coach from the USA.

Looking back, my love for strategy emanated from those teenage beginnings, where to win a game, you had to appreciate your strengths and weaknesses and learn to exploit your opponent through the opportunities he provided.

There was also the team aspect. We played individual games, but we won together and lost together. I encouraged my teammates when they were defeated and celebrated with them when they were victorious. Being the oldest sibling, I already had leadership qualities, and these presented themselves on the tennis team.

Tennis demanded grit.

Mrs. Tlhaphane would refer to my game as erratic, and I grew to hate that label. But since I started the game relatively late, I would crumble when things started heating up in a game. I was short of adequate stroke techniques to cope with some opponents.

Due to my athleticism, I was a "serve and volley" type of player, and my forehand strokes lacked the killer instincts required to win games at high competitive levels. But I was a fighter on the court, not a walkover.

Then, in 1986, we had a visiting professional coach from the US who came to support Mrs. Tlhapane with the elite youth team. My game improved, and he introduced a strategy specifically for my game. "Keep the ball in play," he would shout!

I later got to appreciate what strategy was in the context of corporate: capability that gave one the edge over others. I had done it on the court. Due to his coaching, I started winning more games, even against players who had been with the game for much longer than I had.

My confidence took off, and I enjoyed the game even more. The visiting coach was so impressed with our improvements as the top four team members that he arranged academic scholarships for us to study in the US while pursuing tennis. I did all the tests, including the SAT, and was accepted at the prestigious Phillips Exeter Academy in New Hampshire.

I was over the moon and could picture myself becoming professional and joining the world of the United States as a boy from humble beginnings in Botswana. The school brochure consisted of rolling green grounds, beautiful buildings, and even better, the student ratio was 15 to 1 compared to Botswana's public schools that can go to 40 to 1!

On receiving the acceptance letter, I excitedly told my mother and imagined what life could be like in America. I enjoyed tennis and was good at it, and the idea of playing in another country was exciting. My mother was hesitant about it, though. She talked with her brother, Segale Moiloa, and together, they decided it was best that I didn't accept the scholarship.

They believed that it was risky for me to travel overseas for a tennis scholarship when clearly I was talented academically. It would likely not lead to a secure job, and there would be other opportunities for me to get scholarships or study other subjects that would be more stable.

They emphasized that since I was an "A" student already, I needed to take a risk in other places and that I was still young. In retrospect, I now understand that they were not well-traveled and thought the idea of their son leaving for some unknown lands was too risky. It was in the days before the internet, and they could not Google search and appreciate how great the opportunity was.

After their decision, I had to deliver the news to the visiting coach. He replied, "I am disappointed." I still remember the devastation I felt. It was one of the lowest moments of my life, and at the time, I didn't understand why my mother and uncle were doing this to me.

I could only think about how I was letting the coach down.

He had put so much time into improving my game just for this to happen. From the four of us, two players took the scholarships whilst another player had the same fate as me with his parents.

As difficult as this situation was for me, I learned a lot from the coach. He introduced a new playing tactic of "keeping the ball in play." He encouraged me to practice strokes (forehand, backhand, volleys, serves, etc.) as much as possible until I was consistent.

Being the disciplined fellow I was, I increased my hours on the tennis courts. I spent hours hitting balls against the practice wall if colleagues were not there to practice with. I ingrained this new motto, "Keep the ball in play," into my mindset, which translated to the importance of consistency as an entrepreneur and business leader.

In retrospect, that was the best strategy for me as I lacked depth and "killer edge" with my strokes. The goal was to let my opponents make the mistakes. I had a deep and hard serve that allowed me to get to the net and volley (hit the ball before it bounces on the ground) my way to a win. My strength was agility on the court, and I even loved to dive for volleys at the net, all while tiring out my opponents.

I learned at that early age to play to my strengths. I didn't have a killer backhand, but I did have a good serve. I had to be intentional about a win strategy and put in hours of practice. I was never champion material, but I could compete.

Importantly, I learned that your game can change based on new strategies and having a good coach. The American coach changed me from an "erratic" player to a much more consistent player, and I got to win more games.

The night before tournaments in Harare, the coach would round us up and do pep talks, motivating us to perform the following day. This is a technique I now use with my teams when we are faced with challenges.

I recall my five-set game with Balisa Poncana, who was ranked much higher than me and was one of the older good players at the club. Thanks to the techniques I learned from the American coach, I managed to down him through a five-set showdown. People were surprised at my improvements. Because of the visiting coach's advice and my constant practice, I kept the ball in play.

To win, I needed to fully understand my own strengths and weaknesses and to study the opponent's game so I could exploit any gaps he presented. At the same time, he was doing the same to me. You have to be intentional if you want to win the game.

I would later use this in my businesses and also as a service to clients to provide them with corporate strategy services. Right from the inception of Innolead, I did my homework on positioning in the market, leveraged my strengths, and purposefully drove the business toward a defined vision. All this in a way that was consistent with "keeping the ball in play."

More than the logistical application of my experience with the visiting coach, I had the opportunity to show grit and endurance in a real way. I didn't want this one low moment to ruin tennis for me. It was still a sport I enjoyed and was good at.

Although I didn't understand my mother's decision, I kept working hard and trusted that she meant well. I had to find ways of turning the tears into knowledge.

Tennis was a good foundation for learning strategies and grit and for putting hours into practice to master a skill. With tennis, you are on your own and require no mental and physical prowess. This has been instrumental to my discipline as a student, a corporate worker, and, ultimately, as an entrepreneur. Few things test one's character and grit like entrepreneurship!

My hard work with tennis led me to fun and meaningful experiences later on in life. During my first year at University in the UK, I applied to a summer camp called Kutsher's Sports Academy in the United States. The camp had earned a reputation for professional and recreational sports development in kids to increase their skills in a new or already played sport.

I spent two months coaching children between the ages of seven and fourteen. While coaches and officials came from around the world, I was the only African in the camp, so I was a hit!

The other coaches had not seen anyone else from Africa who could play with such dexterity, and it was clear that people held inaccurate ideas about the continent. But the kids were happily ignorant in a way I found endearing.

They would ask questions about how I learned to play tennis in Africa, and when they wondered if there were any traffic lights in Africa, I joked that we used ostriches to control traffic because they are so tall!

These kids' eyes would sparkle as they listened to me describe my life on the other side of the world. They were eager to step into a new worldview, a concept that was likely unfamiliar to them before.

At this time, I was also studying at the University of Southampton in England and had done various traveling, and I was once again reminded of the invaluable lessons found in new experiences. None of it was easy, but it was unforgettable.

Again, I got to appreciate the value of showing up to different things in life. Experiences bring fun to one's life, help us appreciate different cultures, and build skills required to thrive in today's world.

It was around this time that I started going by Oabona instead of Michael. I had thought about how when African people use Christian names, we alienate ourselves from our culture. I embraced my African heritage and sought to change the stereotypes of the Western world.

People across the world are interested in your unique self, not a colonized version of you. In the end, the name Michael is a foreign name, albeit being given to me under well-meaning circumstances of being baptized under the Catholic Church. My position is that we can still adopt Christianity and other religions, but we do not have to lose our true identity in the process.

Even when I faced challenges, I kept going, not letting low moments define my whole experience. That is what perseverance looked like for me, and it made me so much happier.

The bad things in life are unavoidable, but how you respond is up to you.

The Honey Badger: Nature's Entrepreneur

When you think of the quintessential entrepreneur, you might picture someone who is relentlessly driven, unyieldingly persistent, and astonishingly resilient. But what if I told you that the ultimate embodiment of these traits isn't a person at all but rather a scrappy, fearless, and surprisingly cunning animal—the honey badger?

The honey badger, also known as the ratel, is notorious for its tenacity. It will stop at nothing to achieve its goal, often taking on creatures much larger than itself. Among other places, we can find this animal in the arid bushes of Southern Africa.

Whether raiding a beehive for honey (hence the name) or confronting a venomous snake, the honey badger shows a determination that would put even the most driven entrepreneur to shame. In fact, the Guinness Book of World Records named the honey badger the world's most fearless animal.[8]

Imagine breaking into a hive of aggressive bees, enduring hundreds of stings, and still coming out with the honey. This isn't just a one-time stunt for the honey badger—it's a regular occurrence. Flaps over his ears close during an attack to prevent bees from stinging him there. The honey badger's thick skin and high pain tolerance allow it to withstand the onslaught of bee stings as it pursues its sweet reward.

Entrepreneurs need this kind of tenacity to navigate the treacherous path of starting and running a business. Just like the honey badger, they face numerous challenges and setbacks. However, it's the unyielding pursuit of their goals that sets successful entrepreneurs apart. They don't give up at the first sign of trouble; they dig deeper, just as the honey badger digs through hard ground to reach its prize.

If grit is about passion and perseverance for long-term goals, the honey badger has it in spades. This fearless creature can withstand bee stings, snake bites, and even attacks from larger predators. It has been known to face off against lions, snarling and running backward. It persists in the face of seemingly insurmountable obstacles.

In fact, the honey badger learns from a young age to always stand its ground. The young build up a tolerance to venom by snatching scorpions as snacks. The stings don't stop them from enjoying this delicious treat.

The honey badger is known to take on venomous snakes such as cobras and puff adders. It doesn't just avoid these deadly reptiles; it actively hunts them. In Botswana, there is a particular taste for the large venomous cape cobra, which is found on the arid grassland of South and Western Botswana.

Entrepreneurs need this kind of grit. Building a business is rarely a smooth journey. There will be failures, disappointments, and painful lessons along the way. Those who succeed are the ones who can endure these hardships, learn from them, and keep pushing forward. Like honey badgers, they develop a tough skin that protects them as they navigate the ups and downs of entrepreneurship.

One of the most remarkable traits of the honey badger is its resilience. Even after being bitten by a venomous snake, a honey badger can often recover after a short period of apparent death.

In one documented case, a honey badger was bitten by a puff adder. It collapsed as the venom took effect, lying motionless for several hours. Astonishingly, the honey badger eventually woke up, groggy but alive, and proceeded to eat the snake that had bitten it. This incredible ability to bounce back is a testament to its resilience.

In the world of business, resilience is a crucial trait. Entrepreneurs will face failure. The ability to bounce back, learn from mistakes, and keep moving forward ultimately leads to success. Just as the honey badger doesn't let a snake bite keep it down, entrepreneurs don't let setbacks deter them. They regroup, adapt, and charge back into the fray with renewed vigor.

The honey badger is also known for its intelligence and cunning. It uses tools, works in teams, and has been observed setting traps for its prey. This level of strategic thinking and adaptability is essential for entrepreneurs, who must constantly innovate and pivot to stay ahead in a competitive market.

The Escape Artist: Stoffel the Honey Badger

Let me introduce you to Stoffel, the honey badger who became famous for his incredible escape tactics at a wildlife rehabilitation center in South Africa. Stoffel's escape attempts were nothing short of legendary. He used mud balls to climb over walls, moved rocks to scale fences, and even unlocked gates. No matter how secure his enclosure was made, Stoffel always found a way out.[9]

Entrepreneurs, like honey badgers, must be strategic planners. They must understand their market, anticipate changes, and adapt their strategies accordingly. Whether it's leveraging new technology, pivoting their business model, or outsmarting competitors, entrepreneurs who can think on their feet and adapt to new challenges are the ones who thrive.

Stoffel's clever escapes are a perfect example of the ingenuity and adaptability needed to overcome obstacles and succeed in the business world.

I love the honey badger examples, and in my consulting space, I tend to use animals as examples of grit and strategies for survival. When I watch wild animals, whether in the wild or in national geographic documentaries, I am reminded as to how in the end we are all living with finite lives trying to make the most of Earth.

Embrace Your Inner Honey Badger

The next time you're facing a tough business challenge, remember the honey badger. Embrace its tenacity, grit, resilience, and cunning. Channel your inner honey badger and tackle your obstacles head-on. After all, if a small, scrappy creature can take on lions and venomous snakes, imagine what you can achieve in the world of business!

The Grit of Champions

Michael Jordan is regarded as one of the best basketball players of all time. But you may be surprised to know that he wasn't always at the top. As a sophomore in high school, Michael didn't even make the varsity team. Instead, he saw a spot go to one of his close friends.

In a 1997 Nike commercial, Jordan discussed many of his career failures. At the time, there had been twenty-six times that he was trusted with the game-winning shot and missed. He had missed more than nine thousand shots in his career and lost nearly three hundred games. Now, that number is up to 366 games lost.

Even a great basketball player like him did not do well all the time. As he said, "I've failed over and over and over again. And that is why I succeed." That is true grit!

Jordan retired from basketball three times. The first was shortly after his father was murdered. Soon after, he played baseball for a year and later went back to basketball. After a few more years, he was exhausted, and his coach and several other players retired, so he retired again. He came back a third time for two seasons.

It is clear that Michael Jordan knew when to push on and when to quit. He listened to his body getting tired and understood that his grief was affecting his play. He described losing his passion for the sport after his father's death, and he wasn't going to keep playing if he wasn't into it.

But the important thing is that he didn't let these setbacks stop him permanently. He took the time to deal with them and get back to a better mindset and energy level, and then he got back on the court. You can quit and come back as an entrepreneur. It's a marathon and not a sprint. That's still grit.

A similar story is found in American Olympic gymnast Simone Biles. Her decision to withdraw from the 2020 Tokyo Olympics shocked the world. With her in the lead, the USA team was the team to beat, but her choice was a turning point for athletes everywhere.

After dealing with the stress of the games and the pressure of being the team's star, she stepped back to focus on her mental health. She was open about her experience with the twisties, which happen when a gymnast loses the sense of where they are in midair. Since then, she has been an advocate for mental health.

Her work has certainly paid off. In the 2024 Paris Olympics, she earned three gold and one silver medal, including a gold for individual all-around and another for team all-around. She has openly discussed going to therapy on the day of one of her gold wins to put her in the right mindset, and she said she was having fun, enjoying the sport.

We entrepreneurs face our own version of the twisties. Sometimes, we can look around at our struggling business and lose our sense of where we are and what we're doing. We also may feel the need to retire and take a moment off the court.

There is, however, the flip side of grit, which is knowing when to quit. Being a very obedient person myself, I can have that tendency to carry on in the face of clear signs that it's time to quit. Let's not do that. Listen to your body and prioritize well-being. Your health is the only thing you have.

I showed this virtue when I quit Debswana and when I quit Geoflux. After purchasing a maintenance company called Testmark, it sucked all my time and energy at the expense of valued things like Innolead and my family. It was exhausting and led to clashes with my wife as I would be so low most of the time. It could ruin relationships as well.

I pulled the plug and closed the company with the associated losses and pain to the staff. It is failure that can set you up for future success and build your extra resilience muscles. Surviving failure contributes to future success.

Annie Duke, in her book *Quit,* writes about Mohammed Ali's reluctance to quit when everyone suggested it was time, leading to his neurological decline. Ali also refers to Mount Everest climbers who insisted on persevering to the top when all signs indicated that they should quit, leading to their deaths on their way down the steep slopes.

Grit is seen as courageous, brave, and heroic, while quitting is seen as vice and failure. In reality, they are both important virtues. It is no hero to stay in a bad relationship, stick to a bad business, or run yourself sick mentally and physically. I see especially young entrepreneurs I coach as they drive themselves, too obsessed with achieving success. As entrepreneurs, we need to learn how and when to quit.

We should not be hitting our breaking point, no matter how much we think we need to keep working. I have seen many people sacrifice their health for their business, and trust me, it doesn't end well. I'll share more of those stories in Chapter Eight.

Once we take a step back, though, we need to get back on the court. The version of yourself that will best take your start-up to victory is the one that is refreshed and ready to go for the gold. Grit isn't about pushing yourself until you can't go anymore; it's about knowing how best to handle each challenge so you can secure a long-term win for yourself and your company.

Chapter Takeaways:

- More than talent, it takes grit. You could be the smartest person in the room, but if you don't have the resilience to overcome challenges and the dedication to achieve long-term goals, you won't be successful. Surviving failures builds resilience.

- Activities such as sports help kids build character while they're young. It readies them for later careers and helps them be well-rounded people. Any activity that encourages them to practice and acquire new strategies and skills is beneficial. Exposure builds grit.

- Grit helps you develop passion and perseverance. It is essential for entrepreneurial success, especially when paired with endurance.

- Grit and over-perseverance can be detrimental to one's health and can even kill. Learn when to quit. The opposite of grit, quit is also a virtue. Know when to quit.

PART TWO

THE GIFT OF HAPPINESS

CHAPTER FIVE

JOYREP YOUR LIFE

Happiness is not something ready-made.
It comes from your own actions.
—Dalai Lama

The big wake-up.

I wasn't always committed to happiness. Sometimes, it takes wake-up calls. At forty-seven, I was on top of my health. I remember thinking how lucky I was to not only be so healthy but also to have my parents, wife, great kids, siblings, and friends. My before-bed prayers would include gratitude and appreciation for such blessings.

I had check-ups at the doctor every six months. My doctor couldn't believe my blood tests, which were at optimum readings, including the levels of inflammation, kidney, and the liver. He requested my permission to use these results to show his other patients of the same age that it's possible to be forty-seven and healthy.

I was truly in the prime of my life!

In February 2020, everything changed when a cancer marker appeared positive in my blood tests. A specialist confirmed I had intermediate cancer, and I started radiation treatment in the middle of the pandemic.

This was my first realization that death hovers over us at any time. I thought about how leaving my loved ones so early would be devastating. I started meditating, coming to terms with how little I might have left to live. My entrepreneurial businesses, Innolead, Manenzo, and DigitalGae, would be at risk as I had no plans in place for my absence.

As a disciple of the Strategic Coach program and a natural optimist, I was always looking at 10x growth, spending more time with loved ones, reading more books, traveling the world, and making a higher impact on my society and community. And now this cancer wants to change that!

In the midst of this, I came across the book *The Last Lecture* by Randy Pausch and Jeffrey Zaslow. Pausch had been diagnosed with pancreatic cancer and was given six months to live at forty-eight years old. He had young kids, a wife, a family, and an academic community he loved.

When no one would have blamed him for being upset, he instead demonstrated that with gratitude and positive living, one can remain happy right up to the final day. As a professor at Carnegie Mellon University, he gave an enthusiastic lecture where he reflected on how he lived a happy life despite his terminal disease.

This book hit me hard. This man was around the same age as me and in a similar circumstance. Painful as it was, I appreciated the role of death more, and I slowly accepted that it might be earlier than I planned. Unfortunately, the cancer treatment did not succeed in eliminating the cancer cells, and at the time of writing, I am still battling the disease but am positive that I will defeat the disease.

If there is a positive to the cancer scare, I am determined now more than ever to live true to myself.

Bronnie Ware, who worked in palliative care for many years, wrote a book called *The Five Regrets of the Dying*, where she shares conversations with elderly people on their deathbeds. She summarizes the five regrets as follows:

1. I wish I'd had the courage to live a life true to myself, not the life others expected of me.

2. I wish I hadn't worked so hard.
3. I wish I'd had the courage to express my feelings.
4. I wish I had stayed in touch with my friends.
5. I wish that I had let myself be happier.

Bronnie emphasizes the power of living to one's true self. She shares one interaction with a woman, pseudonym Grace, on her deathbed: "Don't you ever let anyone stop you from doing what you want, Bronnie. How can it be possible that I have waited all these years to be free and independent, and now it's too late?"

We think a lot in terms of what we will do "one day"—travel the world, write a book, change jobs. But we never do any of it. French philosopher Jean-Paul Sartre describes this idea of living according to worldly standards as "bad faith." We are not faithful to our true selves.

Bronnie's work hit me just like Randy's. I was reminded of what's important: connecting with loved ones, living an authentic life, and focusing on happiness. I would become an entrepreneur with happiness at the core, ensuring that what we do as a team is anchored in joy, team-unique abilities, and a compelling purpose.

The more I pursued small, life-giving passions, the more creative I became, benefiting both my personal life and my work.

With all I learned over the past several years, it comes together in this formula that I developed, adapted from Martin Seligman's PERMA model[10] and reframed for entrepreneurs:

JoyReP = Success

This model stands for Joy, Relationships, Engagement, and Purpose. The end product is success. The difference here is that success is not based on material gains and fame. It's the result of taking care of other areas of your life, the heart of well-being. I developed it based on research in philosophy, psychology, neuroscience, and social sciences and largely from the positive psychology movement.

It only takes four simple parts to live well.

Joy

I like to think of joy as finding true fun in life.

Joy is defined by the American Psychological Association as "a feeling of extreme gladness, delight, or exultation ... arising from a sense of well-being or satisfaction."[11]

We experience joy because our bodies release dopamine, a hormone essential for peak performance. The rush makes us feel good, so we crave future dopamine releases.

As neuroscientists Friederike Fabritius and Hans W. Hagemann put it in *The Leading Brain,* "When you have fun, your brain produces dopamine. Without fun, peak performance is practically impossible."

That is where my interest lies: peak performance with fun!

In her book *The Power of Fun,* Catherine Price talks about the importance of fun for a well-lived life. She has created various resources to test how often you experience what she calls True Fun, which is found in the intersection of playfulness, connection, and flow. She reiterates how we've lost the art and science of having fun. I could immediately relate to her saying that. For me, fun should never be postponed until someday in the future!

Based on her model, I have relatively high levels of fun, which makes sense, considering I also score well on happiness questionnaires. Her book was instrumental in helping me see the value of having fun. Her research shows you can only have fun if you take risks, unplug from your phone, and stop caring what others think.

Learning where you find joy is crucial for your mental health. What brings me joy isn't necessarily going to bring you joy and vice versa. For example, I know which friend to call to get me laughing nonstop or which song to blast to boost my mood.

Other fun activities for me include:

- Singing and dancing
- Playing around with kids is a huge mood booster!
- Swimming (although still bad at it!)
- Looking at old pictures, savoring the memories
- Reading a good book
- Enjoying a good meal, such as Botswana's tasty beef or a good cheesecake!
- Walking in nature
- Adventure, like running a farming enterprise in the middle of lion territory.

You may have some of these in common, or you may have to generate your own list. No matter what they are, these fun moments should lift your spirits. You should also pay attention to who you're with, how many people are around you (i.e., if you're in a crowd or just with one person), and if there are any other shared circumstances. For example, I can see themes of moving my body and listening to music in my fun moments.

I fully believe in Socrates' thought that "the unexamined life is not worth living." This is why it's important to be aware of yourself and your joy. As the tests show, I have been able to find joy, and now I want to share that with you.

When we think about fun in our lives, it can be easier to remember it in our childhood. Kids are truly experts in fun! Why? They don't live with the same level of fear that adults do. If you ask a kid what they do for fun, they'll be able to list out activities that they simply enjoy doing. That is why I had such a ball at the Kutsher's Academy sports summer camp with kids!

Adults, however, get caught up in worrying about what others think of them or that they won't be any good at it.

Simply put, a kid would build a blanket fort purely for the thrill and imagination; an adult might be too focused on how sound the structure is. A kid would play in the sand to build castles or tunnels; an adult might be worried about the mess. A kid would jump in puddles because they find it fun; an adult might not want to get muddy or wet.

Get the picture?

Many of the activities we found fun as kids we don't even consider now. When was the last time you played a game of soccer with your friends, bought yourself "kid" toys like Legos or dolls, suggested a game of hide and seek, climbed a tree, or played dress up?

We tell ourselves we can't have the same kind of fun, but is that really true? Whenever I visit my friends, their kids go crazy as we start running around horse playing. They have nicknamed me Uncle Scooby Doo, as I always chase them imitating the cartoon series Scooby Doo.

It's true that you have to take responsibility for your actions now. Your mum isn't there to clean up the mud or sand, and you may not even fit under a blanket fort anymore. But many times, what's really stopping us is our fear. So what if you get muddy? It's better than scrolling on your phone or spending another evening with nothing to do.

When I was a teenager, I formed a dance group with my friends called Crazy Wild Style Jammers. We specialized in break-dance, which was hot in the 1980s. In 1983, I participated in a regional dance competition at the University of Botswana hall with hundreds of university students in attendance. I was 14 years old.

At first, I was afraid of the crowd, imagining how I might mess up and wondering what they would all think of me. Through positive self-talk, I calmed myself down and took control of my emotions. Suddenly, I was completely swept up in the moment, and I forgot about the crowd. My only focus was the fun of the moment. I was lost in the beat of the sounds and the dance moves, and as the crowd went into a frenzy, my dance moves got crazier! I got second place with one of the top breakdance dancers of the time awarded first place.

Have you ever seen a little kid dance in public? They often move how they feel, not noticing who is watching or if they're doing well. In fact, they probably think they're the best dancer in the room! Kids are confident and bold. They don't care what others think; they only do what they want to do, what brings them joy.

In this, I want to be more like a kid!

As you look at your life, give yourself something to look forward to each week or even each day. By making these part of your regular schedule, you'll be having fun without even trying. This should also be applied to your job. Find what about your work makes you the most passionate. Remind yourself why you chose this job in the first place.

When I speak at conferences, I start with a short dance. The crowds go crazy as they join me, and it all starts with a good shot of dopamine for everyone! It has now become my signature start at my speaking assignments.

Also, remember that you don't have to be doing something only if you're good at it. It's possible that your attempt at painting isn't why you've been feeling so dissatisfied; the problem might be how critical you are of your painting skills. You don't have to be van Gogh or Monet!

It may be easier said than done, but don't judge how well you're doing. You're not doing it for fun if you aren't letting yourself *have* fun.

Another type of fun I enjoy is adventure. Although I consider myself a huge adventure man, there is one type that scares me to death. In 1997, I traveled to Victoria Falls for a regional conference. This beautiful waterfall is shared between Zimbabwe and Zambia and is one of the Seven Natural Wonders of Africa. Visitors can go white water rafting, bungee jumping, or take a helicopter tour.

Despite my love of adventure, I couldn't risk jumping with that massive fall and rocks and water waiting! I opted for the helicopter ride and enjoyed amazing views. It was a true once-in-a-lifetime experience that I still think back on decades later. Most of my colleagues did bungee jumping. As for white water rafting, I knew there was no chance I'd choose that because I'm not a good swimmer.

The Lion Story

My favorite adventure is found in nature and wildlife. This is partly what motivated me to go into farming as it provided opportunities to spend time in Botswana's wild bushes that are never short of dangerous animals.

One of our farms is in a lion-infested area. Even before we acquired it in 2008, it was renowned as a playing field for lions. They would come to feed on the cattle, who were easier to kill than the elands, the biggest antelope in the world. A bull can feed twelve to fifteen adult lions.

One time, I went to the farm with my first son, Tshepho, to check on the farm and do some work on the cattle. This Saturday morning, we were by the kraals branding and dipping the cattle.

Our workers were all from the area and are the first people of Botswana, called the San or Basarwa (commonly referred to as bushmen, but this term is no longer appropriate). They occupy vast areas of central and western Botswana and have existed for hundreds of years as hunters and gatherers.

With the push for game reserves and national parks, the Botswana government relocated the San from their original lands, where they lived off hunting. They were placed in newly set up villages with goats and money to start afresh. But since this contradicted their ancestral culture, they resorted to alcohol and remain one of the most marginalized groups in Botswana and perhaps also in Namibia and South Africa.

Now, most farm owners hire them as farmhands and assistants to look after the cattle while we live in cities and towns hundreds of kilometers away. The San are very knowledgeable in these areas, and I learn so much from them, especially the older ones who still possess rich indigenous knowledge.

So, while we were busy tending to the cattle, one of the boys jumped the poles of the kraals and shouted, "It has hit!"

My son and I didn't know what he was talking about, but the rest of the team immediately looked in one direction, where vultures were flying not too far away.

Vultures see when a kill has been made, and they go to the site to scavenge after predators like lions. All around, the guys looked to me for what to do next because this meant lions were on the farm.

Because I was new to this, I asked for their advice, and we agreed that first, we needed to find guns as we did not have one (I later acquired a gun license for the farm, which can be given purely for wild animals).

They told me that one of the neighbors had a gun and was a good shooter. It sounded like Wild West stuff! Despite the risk to the cattle and even to us, my adrenaline was high, and I was very excited!

We gathered a crew of the shooter, other neighbors, and dogs, who chased the lions with their better sense of smell and sight. The dogs led the way with about five guys behind them, including the shooter.

Our 4x4 bakkie (pickup truck) followed, my son driving and me at the back of it with a few confessed cowards as it was relatively safe there. However, there were stories of some lions charging at the bakkie after being shot and injuring people at the back of the truck, so we weren't completely safe.

After tracing the footsteps (spoors), we found that the lions had spent the night about 150 meters from our homestead and had killed an eland that morning.

These guys were amazing at studying the prints and describing exactly what the lions were doing. They could tell that the lions were sitting and watching us before taking off when the dogs started barking. It was almost poetic how these men looked "home" in describing the behavior of the lions.

We went by the fallen eland bull and were shocked to see the blood and little flesh left on the carcass. One could see the teeth marks of the lions as they had ripped through bone and flesh.

The guys could tell the footprints were of two female lions. The eland horn was attractive to me, and I requested that the guys take them, but they were quick to remind me that it's illegal. Poaching was outlawed to protect the animals, and taking the horn would also be considered against the law.

The San people loved hunting, and the wildlife officers had a history of terrorizing them whenever they saw them with game meat as they thought they hunted illegally. I could tell by the way the team was going around the carcass that they were both excited to see the kill and terrified at the same time.

We chased the lions for another four hours across many farms and found they ran back to the Central Kalahari Game Reserve, a wildlife protected area where it is illegal to chase or shoot them.

For me, this is a real adventure, having a great experience with our staff and learning so much amid some scary moments with lions. Other wild animals that regularly feed on our animals are wild dogs, leopards, cheetahs, and brown hyenas. Botswana also has many dangerous snake varieties.

I love snakes (at a distance), and seeing one at the farm is always a treat! I have encountered black mambas, rock pythons, boom slangs, cape cobras, and puff adders. The mamba is the number one killer of cattle among all the snakes—and the most feared. The farm workers are always proud when they manage to kill one.

As a conservationist, I never like it when they kill the snakes as one day we will run out of these fantastic animals. Only once did I succeed in stopping them from killing a python that had killed our chickens and was so full it could not move.

When I arrived at the farm, it was lying motionless by our farmhouse. I instructed them to put it in a sack and throw it a few kilometers away. They were not happy, but I did teach them a bit about conservation and the need to strike a balance with these animals.

As you can see, I find adventure and being outdoors thrilling! The farm has allowed me to pursue both of these, and I find much joy in being among the wildlife and plants, whether working with my cattle, chasing away lions, or mixing entrepreneurship with fun.

Entrepreneurs have the unique power not only to design what their jobs will look like but also to influence the jobs of others. By discovering what brings our employees joy, we can help them live happier lives at work.

At Innolead, we started a staff club called iGlow, which is fully charged with identifying and implementing fun activities for the team. It's a wonder to watch team members design their own fun activities and develop a strong sense of belonging and team connection, which is fundamental for a high-paced consulting environment with high stress levels.

In my thirty years of working, I have always attempted to add fun to the work I do. In the 90s, I worked as a section engineer in the Debswana mines, where I led a team of maintenance engineers.

Most bosses stayed away from subordinates, but I would shock my teams by attending their social gatherings. They loved to discover firsthand that I'm human just like them. It made me a better leader because they grew in respect for me, and we enjoyed working together more.

Also, while I was working at the mine, I started a church choir called "Melodi ya Jwana" ("the melodies of diamond-bearing rocks") as part of maintaining my happiness, at the same time creating fun for dozens of Jwaneng town community members as we practiced, laughed, and performed together around Botswana.

Finding these moments of joy made the biggest difference for me. I always have things to look forward to. This doesn't mean I don't face roadblocks, but these challenges are easier to face when I'm looking through the lens of a joy-filled life.

So, as an entrepreneur, what is your true joy formula? Take a fun audit. Your body and mind can only operate at peak performance when you find your joy formula. Make it part of your week plan and take time to identify what fun means to you. It's part of the inside job.

Turn on your fun gene that has been lying buried! The results are cool.

Questions: Evaluating Joy

What are some activities that bring you joy?

1. _____

2. _____

3. _____

4. _____

5. _____

How can you include more of these activities in your life? What priorities do you need to change in order to pursue joy?

_____

_____

_____

Relationships

As Aristotle said, we are social animals. Go alone to a big city and you'll see that you can be surrounded by people and still feel lonely. Even the moments of fun from above are most effective in the company of others.

Thus, relationships naturally follow Joy in this JoyReP philosophy. As we'll discuss in Chapter Seven, African ideology affirms that no one exists in isolation. This is why people across the world are feeling lonely. They try to reach success without connecting with their community, and they end up unhappy.

Entrepreneurship, by its nature, is a lonely and solitary affair. We burn the midnight oil founding companies, building pitch decks, and being rejected by potential funders. Google's founders were rejected 260 times before making a breakthrough! It can be daunting when approached in a lonesome way.

But loneliness is everywhere. During her time as Prime Minister of the UK, Theresa May appointed a Minister of Loneliness after a report that said roughly nine million British citizens were lonely. Loneliness is a big issue!

One study compared smoking to loneliness and, in a meta-analysis, found that the mortality risk for loneliness is the same as smoking fifteen cigarettes a day.[12]

The desire for strong relationships should not be shocking. Friendships have been highlighted in the media for generations: Frodo and Sam; Harry, Ron, and Hermione; Han Solo and Chewbacca; Thelma and Louise; Sherlock Holmes and Dr. Watson; Spock and Kirk—the list goes on!

We remember our closest relationships in little ways. For example, I could recognize my mother's smell as soon as I walked into my house. It was a comforting reminder of home.

As I mentioned before, my mother would often take me along on her frequent visits with friends and family. Although I did not appreciate these boring visits as a kid, I am so grateful for them now because they have given me treasured relationships I have to this day.

My mother's support system during her divorce and her struggles with raising us came from her siblings and friends. She had tight, healthy relationships and invested time to visit them over tea, burning hours on hours just talking and connecting. Her typical Saturday afternoon was either her visiting friends or us hosting family. It is part of our African heritage.

Through one of Mum's friends, Mrs. Kgobe, I developed a close friendship with her son, Lesibane Kgobe. We became best friends as early as Standard One when we lived in Selebi-Phikwe, where both our parents worked at the time. We were exactly the same age.

Our parents bonded because they were both from South Africa and were both teachers. When my family moved to Gaborone in 1977, my friendship with Lesibane ended, though we occasionally exchanged letters.

Then, out of the blue in 1979, our teacher announced that a new student was joining our class, and in walked Lesibane! This was one of the best feelings ever, seeing a long-lost friend for the first time in years. I remember smiling to myself with the feeling of pure joy. It was an incredible feeling that now reminds me how key friendship is to happiness.

It did not take much for our friendship to blossom again. We ate together during breaks, walked together after school, went to movies, played on weekends, and visited each other with our families. I have to add that they had a much bigger house with electricity and a TV, so I would insist on visiting them any chance I got so I could watch some TV!

This was one of my early relationships that instilled in me the importance of friends.

One of the longest studies that shows the impact of relationships is the Harvard Study of Adult Development, which started in 1938.[13] These men were surveyed over the course of their lives to determine what makes people healthy and happy. In the group were 268 Harvard sophomores and 456 disadvantaged boys from Boston.

The study included questionnaires, physical and mental check-ups, and interviews with them and their families. The results were clear: the quality of relationships was crucial for a happy and healthy lifespan. People who are connected live longer.

Although the study started with just men, it expanded to include the families of the original participants. Relationships were found to be more helpful for happiness than wealth and even genes.

The quantity of relationships is not nearly as important as quality. Anyone who has been divorced can tell you it's not just about being married; having a healthy and fulfilling marriage is what creates a meaningful relationship.

While I was studying engineering in England, I grew competitive with four English boys at the top of the class. These were nice guys who I am sure I could have been friends with, but instead, I kept my distance from them. I was a bit intimidated as they not only got top marks in class but also hung around with very attractive girls!

In the end, my competitive attitude caused me to lose out on potential friends, and I still wonder what could have been had I been brave enough to approach them and explore friendship. Don't miss an opportunity to start new friend-ships when it comes by.

Despite this, I remained committed to familial relation-ships as I sent money back home, and I sponsored my mom and uncle to come to my graduation. It was one of my most memorable times, hosting my mother, uncle and aunt in England for a couple of weeks. They got to meet my friends and visited different tourist places together, like Buckingham Palace and the Isle of Man.

I also had a strong group of friends from my earlier uni-versity days in Botswana. Trouble came when I was working as an engineer at the mines after graduation, and I stopped spending time with my friends.

I'll never forget when one of my best friends from my days at the University of Southampton invited me to his wedding. I was close with both him and his wife (we shared an apartment in Southampton for three years) and he wanted me to be his best man, a great honor!

But instead of saying yes, I decided I couldn't spare that much time away from work per my workaholic attitude. It is a choice I regret to this day. I was isolating myself.

Fortunately, we later connected, and every time we visited England, we stayed at their place in London. They also became guardian parents to our son Motheo when he was studying for his degree in England. He had a "home away from home" and would spend weekends with them and their two lovely kids. It's never too late to reconnect with old friends.

According to the American Psychological Association's 2022 Stress in America survey, 46% of Americans under thirty-five said that most days, they are so stressed they can't function.[14] This number was even worse for Black Americans under thirty-five, 56% of whom agreed with the statement. For all individuals ages thirty-five to forty-four, this number was 42%. This might be a survey from America, but this kind of stress happens all over the world!

What does this have to do with relationships?

Several studies have shown the positive effect of relationships on stress. One such article shows that social support is directly related to a person's resilience in the face of stress.[15] The more connected we are with people who can encourage us in our difficulties, the better equipped we are to bounce back.

I have seen proof of this in my own life. In my thirties, I became a burnt out, lonely entrepreneur. I was a classic workaholic burning sixty to seventy hours per week. I came home so exhausted I had no energy to spend time with my wife, Nancy, and my boys. I'd collapse on the sofa, have dinner, watch a bit of TV, and then go off to bed to do the same the next day. I lost sleep to days spent worrying about work. I was losing my bubbly and fun-loving self.

When I finally saw the negative impact of my struggling relationships, I knew I had to make some profound changes. I invited my friends and their wives to get together on Valentine's Day. Some of their wives were shocked to see me, especially if I hadn't been to their weddings. We were never as noisy as we were that day, even getting reprimanded by the hotel!

Now, I make time for monthly get-togethers with friends, going hunting, or relaxing around a fire. We have an annual weekend out at the farm to connect in a relaxed nature setup. It's one of my best times of the year and is great to look forward to on a yearly basis. We would come back from the farm fully rejuvenated.

Despite our closeness, it can be hard for men to talk about the important stuff, like health problems or relationship issues. Encouraging one friend to go to the doctor more often to monitor his chronic health condition was a big step toward open communication. We as a group have worked on being truly vulnerable with each other about the big challenges in our lives. We keep getting better, and that's the key.

Another important side of relationships is in the workplace. As an entrepreneur, it's important for me to have a team I can rely on, and it's equally important for them to feel like they can trust me. I try to be honest with them about what's happening behind the scenes, just as I hope they know they can come to me if they need anything.

Have you ever had a day at work where you felt like you had no idea what was going on? Maybe you were the last to be looped in on an important update or your co-worker left out important details on your latest assignment. No matter what happens, it's frustrating. The ability to connect well with staff is one of the best feelings at work, and it takes a leader to loosen up and be vulnerable. Being vulnerable does not translate to weakness.

You should communicate with your team as much as you can. No one wants to feel like they're hearing something last minute, and they shouldn't have to be guessing at your expectations. Not appropriately keeping your employees in the loop is going to create more conflict and more work for you, and it could take a toll on your relationship with them. Healthy relationships with co-workers are a key part of everyone's well-being and happiness.

It can be extremely lonely as an entrepreneur, and employees still see you as unable to become a friend as the last man in the hierarchy. They all look to you for guidance during tough times and good times and can find it difficult to connect with you at a personal level.

I try to become truly human in their eyes. I readily apologize when I have been wrong and have conversations with them at personal levels. They are my tribe, and that's where I belong. They can also support me when things are tough. I have shared with them my personal health concerns, and it's great when some of them keep checking on me.

If you run into an issue, talking it over with your employees can even help you find a solution. Someone could have the perfect suggestion that you never would have thought of. There's a reason you're called a "team."

Collaboration is part of the description. An accessible and good relationship with staff provides "psychological safety" and allows them to freely express themselves, be happy, and as a result, be more productive and become better leaders themselves.

Communication is not just good when problems arise; it's a relationship builder and the lifeblood of any organization.

I would go to the extent of recommending that social skills be taught at schools as a life skill. Kids should be taught how to make friends and interact with family and other people. We have technologies, such as social media, that are working against social interactions, and introducing such skills in schools would mitigate that.

We would be creating a better world!

Questions: Evaluating Relationships

Where do you fall on this scale?

Lonely————————————————————Connected

Why?

_____

_____

Name 2 specific ways you will invest in a relationship this week.

1. _____

_____

2. _____

_____

Engagement

As human beings, we all need engaging work. We can try to stumble through a job we don't really like, but we'll never feel satisfied. Engagement follows Relationships in JoyReP. The formula would be incomplete without a vocation that occupies us on an ongoing basis.

Hungarian philosopher Mihaly Csikszentmihalyi researched a concept he called "flow." This is a state of total concentration on one activity. It's being so pulled into a good book that you stay up late into the night or focusing so intently on your work that hours pass without you realizing.

This can also be described as being "in the zone." It happens when your superior skills meet the right level of challenge and time seems to stop.

This idea can be seen with athletes like Serena Williams. She has talked about being completely absorbed in every tennis match, giving little attention to anything other than the court, the ball, and her opponent. She shuts down her mind, allowing only calming or motivating thoughts so she can hype herself up and stay focused.

With the right skills and a clear passion, anyone can enter a flow state. As shown by Serena, we first have to get rid of any distractions, both internal and external. No phones or negative self-talk can disrupt your focus.

The concept of flow is reflected in other cultures. In Chinese philosophy, Dao has a concept called *Wu Wei*. It is commonly described as "effortless action." Think back to my experience in my dance group when I was able to enjoy myself by being caught in the music. I even forgot there was a crowd as I got lost in the dance moves.

When I was imagining how I might mess up, I was overworking myself, but after I stopped to simply embrace the moment, I was effortless in the moment, no longer thinking about what I was doing but simply letting it happen.

Wu wei is like breathing. We don't often make a conscious effort to breathe in and out; it happens naturally. Your body is capable of filling your lungs without you having to tell yourself to do so.

In this way, embracing wu wei is like being in flow. You don't overthink or focus on the negatives, you only do what feels right in each moment. What is most important is the here and now.

Often, when you are in flow, you are leaning into your intuition. You won't typically have to stop and think about your next move. If you do have to plan ahead, this process itself, like figuring out a puzzle, could be part of flow for you. Some people hate making plans, but others thrive on it.

According to the Flow Research Collective, there are twenty-two flow triggers, ranging from "clear goals" and "sense of control" to "spite" and "shared risk."[16] These factors can set off or trigger the flow state by creating the unique conditions each person needs to be engaged in.

Many of the flow triggers can lead to an increase in dopamine, which is part of the flow state. Imagine you check something off your to-do list. You feel accomplished with a small dose of dopamine. Now imagine you mark several things off your list in a short amount of time. Those continuous dopamine hits can contribute to a flow state.

When I speak at conferences on my favorite topics like leadership, happiness, and 10x technologies, I usually get lost in "flow," and almost all the time, I get into trouble with time allocated! When fully absorbed in my tennis games all those years ago, time would just fly, fully present and in a state of flow.

My best places for writing this book were at the farm, where I work in a natural environment in peace and calm. The regular deep sleep I have there also contributes to extra creativity and enjoyment of the task. Every morning, I start with a cup of coffee in the garden and fifteen minutes of reading. The garden with its seasonality, the sun and the trees all around make my day start on a bright note.

Though British actress Emily Blunt has not used the word flow, it is evident in her work that she knows what it means to be engaged. In *The Devil Wears Prada*, her big break movie, she improvised many of her lines, a clear sign that she was focused on the scene and in tune with her character.

In another of her films, *A Quiet Place*, one of her iconic scenes involves her character giving birth in a bathtub while surrounded by creatures that attack when anyone makes a noise. This scene, considered one of the most memorable and nerve-wracking of the movie, was done in one take. Her performance was so stellar that the members of the crew were upset after witnessing the scene.

Emily Blunt's work shows the importance of surrendering to the moment. She went with the flow of the scene to improvise lines, staying aware of what was going on around her and trusting her instincts.

Her example teaches us that flow is not just reserved for an actor on set, just as Serena Williams shows that it's not just for an athlete on the court. Anyone can be in flow anywhere they are. Entrepreneurs can be engaged at a desk, in a meeting, or building a product by hand. What puts you in flow will be different than your peers, but the one sure thing is that you *can* be in it.

That being said, you won't always be in flow. Certain activities, while completely necessary, might be boring. Ideally, delegate those tasks to team members who enjoy them, but sometimes, you have to suck it up and get those assignments done yourself. Otherwise, note what tasks keep you engaged and energized so you can include them in your schedule.

Many people are pursuing careers that don't align with their skills, and by the time they realize their mistake, they feel like it's too late. As Annie Duke says in her book *Quit*, "When your identity is what you do, then what you do becomes hard to abandon, because it means quitting who you are." In other words, people's identities are so wrapped up in what they do that they feel it would be wrong to quit.

As entrepreneurs during start-up phases, we have to cover many aspects of the business, even ones we'd rather not do. I had to do accounts, sales, people management, product development, and client meetings. And I don't like accounts and dealing with numbers despite passing my engineering degree!

I won't quit farming or management consulting soon because they align with who I am. I also love the freedom of expressing myself through my business venture, working with people, and impacting lives in a positive way. It makes me happy, and that is why engagement is part of the JoyReP formula.

In my thirty years of corporate and entrepreneurial work, I have seen how unfulfilling work can suck life out of people. We force ourselves into jobs where we aren't happy, whether for money, fear of the unknown, or even laziness.

By discovering our skills and learning how to apply them—whether in our current job or a new one—we can learn to be engaged in our work, finding what activities bring us to our flow state so we can find true happiness and fulfillment.

Questions: Evaluating Engagement

What are some activities or work where you feel in flow? (If you can't think of anything, pay attention and think about it over the next week.)

1. _____
2. _____
3. _____
4. _____
5. _____

What do these activities have in common? (ie. With certain people, a calm or energetic activity, at work or at home, etc.)

_____
_____
_____
_____

Purpose

A purpose is the reason why we do what we do. It motivates you even when life gets difficult, and it helps you feel fulfilled. Without a purpose, you'll lack direction, and the happiness formula will be incomplete. It connects the present to the future by giving you a goal to live for. Joy, relationships, and engagement without a sense of true North or meaning would shortchange your happiness and, ultimately, your success.

Purpose is a familiar concept, popularized by self-help books and leaders like Nietzsche, who said, "Where there is why, one can bear any how." Without a reason why, we will feel lost in life and directionless.

Viktor Frankl wrote *Man's Search for Meaning* about finding purpose. He details the horrors he experienced in a concentration camp during World War II and how, even in horrible situations, people can find meaning in their suffering.

Viktor lost his family, including his pregnant wife, in the camps, but he returned to Vienna after the war so he could further study psychiatry. He remained passionate about man's search for meaning. Whilst most of his counterparts in the camps succumbed to the horrible conditions and died, his "true north" and clarity of his purpose contributed to his survival.

Viktor proves we all need a purpose.

When I was younger, I was involved in the Boy Scouts movement. I still remember the oath vividly:

"On my honor, I promise that I will do my best to do my duty to God and my country, to help other people, and to keep the Scout Law."

I learned the importance of grit, resilience, and purpose. We were grilled on the oath at all the meetings. The merit-based advancements between levels encouraged me to excel as I knew it was up to me to make progress.

Playing dumbbells in the Scout band, I found a sense of belonging and, even stronger, purpose. The band even played at Botswana's 10th anniversary independence celebrations in the Copper mine town of Selebi-Phikwe where we lived at the time in 1976. It felt like there was meaning behind our performance at that tender age of 7 years.

Your purpose helps you see your potential for growth. If you have an opportunity that contradicts your purpose, you'll know you shouldn't accept it. Your purpose is unique to you, so no one can tell you what it should be. If everyone had the same purpose, we would not have the revolutionary thinkers who changed the way things are.

The Greek word *Meraki* describes the surrender of putting yourself into your work or doing something with your soul. You are engulfed in a meditative calm as you do what you love, similar to the flow state.

After high school, I went through a mandatory year-long national service program called *Tirelo Sechaba*. I was stationed at Pilikwe, the same village the first president's uncle, Tshekedi Khama, founded after he opposed Seretse and Ruth's marriage. Thus, the village was full of history and heritage.

The most beneficial volunteer position I had was as an administrator at the *kgotla*, the traditional Tswana community council meeting, where cases were presented before the *kgosi*, the chief. Through listening to the cases, I stayed informed on social issues and local conflicts.

One case had a particular impact on me. A man evaded arrest after stealing a bull, and when we eventually found him, he was charged with "disobedience of lawful order" according to the Penal Code of Botswana. Before even being charged with theft, he was sentenced to nine months imprisonment for evading arrest.

I watched the old man get into the back of the van, no lawyer or representation. Although I support tradition, I found it incredibly unfair, particularly because at the time, there were cases of land grabs by politicians, and one of the Ministers was sentenced to six months.

Because this old man had no representation, he went to prison longer for a less severe crime and still had to answer later for a crime that could add two years to his sentence. My eyes were opened to the social inequality in the justice system. I feel partly responsible for this injustice that was just executed before my eyes but was helpless to do anything as I was still a student.

This experience helped me realize my purpose: helping people. I loved getting connected to the community through things like the choir and the soccer team in the village. I showed up, and this enriched my stay at the village. I volunteered at the clinic and in the school. My focus was on how I could support those around me.

My experience reminded me of the American Peace Corps system, where Americans are seconded for a year, volunteering to live in Botswana villages under host families. Many have had life-changing experiences, some even deciding to return and live in Botswana for the rest of their lives.

The experience cemented my love for my country and a sense of purpose for my career later to contribute to the upliftment of our people.

Years into my work at the Debswana mines, I knew it was time to leave. I was growing in a way that Debswana was not able or willing to support me. My purpose was not aligned with the Debswana vision as I had to tell the De Beers Group leadership panel that guided our career paths. My subsequent meeting with the Debswana company managing director, Mr. Louis Nchindo, who disagreed with my ambitions for Debswana, finally sealed my fate.

If what I saw as my purpose could not be endorsed by the highest office in the company, then there was no need to stay. It was time to define my destiny, and so I decided to leave the company. I had to quit so I could pursue my purpose in life, which was highly important for my happiness.

It was a bold move to leave a prestigious salaried job, company car, manager's house, and other fringe benefits like subsidized education support for kids. But walking from the managing director's office, my decisions were crystal clear: this was not my home.

As fate would have it, I got a call from one of the most successful Botswana consulting companies at the time, Geoflux. The company's managing director was head-hunting me for a role where I would become part of the company's future growth at the equity level. I bought into the company's vision, which offered consulting services in geology, hydrogeology, and environmental services. My purpose was not being fulfilled at Debswana, and it was time to leave.

When I joined the Geoflux team, I was the Director of the Mechanical and Electrical Engineering consulting services arm. Starting the electrical-mechanical division with just one other person was a big challenge. We designed engineering infrastructure, supervised contractors, and engaged clients. My first experience with a start-up was just as the division was new, with ambitious growth targets.

Years later, while working in Johannesburg as an engineering consultant for Debswana based at De Beers offices, a presentation at a conference from a South African-based X-Pert Group (one of the leading project management firms in South Africa at the time) company director inspired my entrepreneurial spirit.

The company specialized in project management, and I could use the concepts of project management to assist my country in executing the many excellent policies that we were renowned for but failed to implement. I immediately approached the director on the edges of the conference, expressed my desires, and later met the CEO, Mr. Clinton in't Veld, who agreed to partner for the Botswana market.

I planned to leave Geoflux to pursue this new purpose of starting X-Pert Group in Botswana as a franchise, but my colleagues encouraged me to stay on and rather take over X-Pert under Geoflux as part shareholder. A second start-up experience kicked in as I now had to develop project management and other management services products and grow the business, which I did with our team.

This experience taught me how much I enjoyed helping businesses grow, compete, innovate, and contribute to our economy. In 2009, I transformed X-Pert Botswana to Innolead Consulting as we could run the company independently outside a franchise arrangement.

A franchise arrangement can help in learning the ropes of running a business as you learn the mother company processes, but I desired to be free and to chart my own company my way. It was a new, exciting journey, and we worked with many companies in Botswana and the region, strengthening their performances and sustainability and, in the process, contributing to our Africa growth ambitions.

A new chapter was opened, chasing my passion and my purpose in life. I seek to transform businesses and support our government agencies to be more efficient and competitive and positively impact the lives of our people.

Marie Curie lived in poverty as a young Polish student studying in Paris. To survive harsh winters, she had to pile all her clothes on top of her at night because she rarely had enough coal to power her stove. She typically ate bread and chocolate, eggs, or fruit. Because she was academically behind the French students due to her Polish education, she had to do a lot of personal study to catch up.

Despite this, she enthusiastically pursued her studies. She would spend hours studying in the library or working in her room late into the night. In her book, *Pierre Curie*, she wrote that this time, "All that I saw and learned that was new delighted me. It was like a new world opened to me, the world of science, which I was finally permitted to know in all liberty."

She found incredible purpose in science. At a time when women rarely pursued higher education, she was the first woman in France to receive a doctorate.

The same year, she, her husband, and another man received a Nobel Prize for their work in radiation. She was the first woman to receive a Nobel Prize. Later was the first person to receive one twice and the only one to receive one in two different sciences.

It is believed that Marie Curie did not fully understand the risks radiation posed to her health, but we can wonder if that would have changed her passion.

She began researching radiation as a possible cure for cancer. After discovering the element radium, she refused to patent the radium refining process so it could be used freely, even though it would have made her rich. Her passion for science influenced her daughter to study chemistry, making the Curies the family with the most Nobel Prizes.

Marie Curie even paused her research during World War I to bring mobile X-ray devices to the front lines. She personally drove the apparatus and worked close to the front line so she could help the injured soldiers.

Marie Curie worked with purpose. She was driven by the idea of helping people, whether it be through cancer treatment or on the battlefield, and she was passionate about her work in the sciences. She paved the way for men and women alike to study radiation and chemistry.

If we all pursue our purpose even half as much as Marie Curie, we would be making a difference. As the saying goes, "Who you are is why you are here." Nothing is as liberating as living your authentic self. As an entrepreneur, punctuate your life with a clear sense of purpose. Take time to frame it and write it down, and that will become your reason for living. That will give you extra fuel to drive and succeed in your enterprise.

My core purpose is "To positively impact lives in Africa through leveraging insights and 10x technologies." And I do this following the JoyReP formula.

Questions: Evaluating Purpose

Your purpose may change for different areas of life. Choose one aspect (work, family, home, hobbies, etc.) and brainstorm your purpose for doing it. This will be what motivates you to dedicate yourself to it.

Consider these questions:

- **What about this ignites your passion?**
- **What are your strengths and skills?**
- **What are your values / moral code?**
- **What kind of legacy do you want to leave behind?**

_____

_____

_____

_____

Write yourself a mission statement using your purpose and your goals.

_____

_____

Success

Many people believe that to be happy, you first need to be successful. They say once you're the CEO of a multi-million dollar company or on the "40 Under 40" list, you can finally relax and focus on the cheerful side of life.

This is the opposite of the truth. Tony Robbins' interview with billionaires bears testimony to this.[17] The majority were unhappy despite being famous and materially rich.

By pursuing Joy, Relationships, Engagement, and Purpose, you get a solid feeling of real and impactful accomplishment. But we see most entrepreneurs pursuing success and winning for winning's sake.

When you pursue success without joy, without maintaining supporting relationships, and without work that does not fit well with your talents—it's bound to be empty! We now have well-documented case studies to prove this: Brian Chesky, Mo Gawdat, Trevor Noah, Kate Spade, and many others discussed in this book. I have also experienced and seen it with my eyes. Money and fame don't bring happiness.

These four components in the JoyReP concept are the steps on your path to a happy life. Each part has to be balanced and work together in harmony. Otherwise, certain areas of your life will be overlooked.

It's time to JoyReP your life to achieve fulfilling and authentic success. You deserve this.

Chapter Takeaways:

- Find joy in your daily activities. Take your happiness audit and use JoyReP to uplift your happiness level.
- Build meaningful relationships. Call and meet a friend you haven't talked to in years, connect with a cousin, or visit an elderly relative. It's enriching and can broaden

your social support. Isolation and loneliness are becoming a new epidemic.

- I highly recommend Bronnie Ware's book, *Five Regrets of the Dying*. Read it, and it will help you stop postponing your life's essentials, like friends, and teach you to live a life true to yourself.

- Write down your purpose statement and live by it daily. It supports you through hardships and the dark valleys of entrepreneurship.

CHAPTER SIX

ENTREHAPPINESS

Happiness is the secret ingredient for successful businesses. If you have a happy company, it will be invincible.
—Richard Branson, co-founder of Virgin Group

If there's one thing I've learned throughout my life, happiness is an inside job. No one can define what it means or looks like for you. It comes from within. You will never feel fully successful if you are not happy.

Some people strive their entire lives for the next big achievement, and even after the dream promotion, the "perfect" spouse, and the most expensive houses and cars, they are shocked to discover it's only fleeting. It's what the experts call "the myths of happiness," which so many of us live by.

When your brain is in the correct mode of positivity, true success will follow. Otherwise, you will face disappointment. Remember JoyReP, and real, fulfilling success will follow.

According to Harvard professor and happiness expert Arthur Brooks, happiness is not the absence of unhappiness. Instead, moments of sadness, anger, and fear are necessary for human survival and growth. We must be able to understand ourselves and turn negative situations into positive ones.

I wonder why such basic human emotions bring so much despair to our lives. We were never taught the skills to find happiness amidst our challenges. The church played a significant role in teaching morality and virtues, but joy was on the peripherals of mainstream education.

People tend to classify happiness in terms of short-term pleasure, but true happiness is long-term and holistic. It seems absurd that one of the most critical aspects of human life receives little attention on a global scale.

Despite this past tendency, we have seen an exponential rise in happiness research in recent years. Self-help books are flying off the shelves, and podcasts have substantial global followings. As humans, we all aspire to be happy. In Africa, we dominate the bottom rankings of the UN World Happiness Reports.[18] Entrepreneurs are particularly affected as it is a demanding occupation that can lead to depression, substance use, and loneliness.

This intersection where happiness meets entrepreneurship is EntreHappiness.

According to many studies, happy people make better leaders, earn more money, are more social, are more likely to get and stay married, and have better immune systems and higher life expectancies. They have lower stress levels, stronger relationships, a healthier heart, and increased productivity. In short, they're well-rounded and relaxed people, just what entrepreneurs need to stay vibrant, creative, and resilient.[19] [20]

With so many benefits, why wouldn't you want to be happy? Choosing happiness when there are many reasons to be upset means you can bounce back when life throws problems your way.

EntreHappiness is the strategy I created for entrepreneurs to live happier lives. We deserve happy lives so we can enjoy the amazing benefits of happiness, as illustrated above. Before we get into those eight steps, let's break down the two parts of EntreHappiness: Entrepreneurship and Happiness.

Introducing Entrepreneurship

The United States is one of the wealthiest countries in the world.

Its economy allows entrepreneurs to thrive, from the Rockefellers and Henry Ford to modern Elon Musk. The USA Silicon Valley is the best example of a place where ideas are generated, start-ups flourish, and billionaires are built.

In *Innovation and Entrepreneurship*, Peter Drucker talks about how the American economy showed a huge job growth of 40 million people from 1965 to 1985 despite inflation, oil shocks, recessions, and major job losses.

The best and most straightforward definition of entrepreneurship is by the Frenchman Jean-Baptiste Say in 1800, "The entrepreneur shifts economic resources out of an area of lower and into an area of higher productivity and greater yield." So, creating many entrepreneurs boosts the economy.

An entrepreneur creates a venture or business model that creates value for society and gets a return in the form of profits. Management guru Peter Drucker says that entrepreneurs do not just do something better but differently.

Entrepreneurs build their businesses on a bigger future and are not blocked from their goals by any suffocating systems. We are free to enjoy the freedom to be who we are in a way that adds value to society!

Once I discovered I could not fit in a corporate setting, my decision to quit was clear. It was what is called an intrinsic goal, an idea that comes out of the field called self-determination theory.

Intrinsic motivation comes internally from personal success and psychological needs. On the other hand, extrinsic motivation comes from the outside world's priorities, like money and social recognition.

Intrinsic goals drive true entrepreneurs. They are powered by the inner self, an internal operating system that desires to grow and add value for its own sake. That was me when I left the mine, joined Geoflux, started X-Pert Group and then Innolead, started the farming enterprise, started the technology company DigitalGae, and later launched an AI company called OrionX. It's my inner game at play while I pursue my purpose, underlined by JoyReP.

In Africa, we have started building self-made billionaire entrepreneurs like Strive Masiyiwa of Liquid Intelligence, Adrian Gore of Discovery Health, and Patrice Motsepe of African Rainbow Minerals. We need to make this pervasive across Africa by solving our grand challenges. Africa will leapfrog only if we develop a cadre of world-class entrepreneurs across the breadth and depth of the continent in millions.

There is one big question I have pondered for many years: is entrepreneurship a calling? Is there some spiritual aspect to venturing that adds value to society?

Some theologians and philosophers believe so, and I tend to agree with them.

Max Weber particularly stands out as the sociologist who was fascinated by why religion seemed to be a significant factor in determining levels of wealth.[21] He believed that the spirit of capitalism is not greed or excessive consumption but the creation of order and the best use of resources. And that the protestant movement was behind the rise in the development of Northern European countries, which became the richest block in the world at the time.

For those with a calling like entrepreneurship, there is no problem in reconciling the spiritual and economic aspects of life. When nations build wealth, people's quality of life improves, and citizens become happier.

So, are we playing a "godly" role by contributing to growing economies and employment and making people materially and mentally better? My answer is yes!

We may not deliberately turn our ventures or knowingly express our spiritual energies through work for the betterment of the world, but I believe there is grace to what we do that I have, over the years, struggled to describe!

Employing and engaging people in work they love, contributing taxes to elevate people from poverty, and improving national and global happiness through entrepreneurial activities have a godly spirit to them.

Weber's theory aligns very much with the message of this book; capitalism and entrepreneurship are not about the mad rush to spend and consume for worldly pleasures but about the creation of wealth through the good use of resources and adding value to society.

When I sat with the dozens of entrepreneurs at Strategic Coach in Toronto, I pondered the millions of dollars in net worth of those men and women. I realized it's not about their wealth, it's the difference they have made in society in finance, agriculture, health, and technology.

Then, the feeling of grace captured me, and I became grateful to be part of this lot. It's humbling and gives me extra batteries to run on!

The scriptures themselves support the role of happiness in society and how essential it is for man. As Psalm 68:3 says, "The godly are happy; they rejoice before God and are overcome with joy" (NET). As discussed under JoyReP, being joyful and happy makes you a much more productive member of society.

I have often been overwhelmed by gratitude whenever I recover from very daunting challenges in our businesses—recovering from a bad drought in 2017 and 2018 when we lost many cattle, surviving the 2008 financial crash, deciding to shut down a company I had acquired because it was causing me pain and draining our resources. I have surmounted all of these obstacles.

When you make it out of such calamities and have many more years of flourishing and employing more people, you can only be grateful and label this a calling, as only a few of us can steer our ships through these stormy seas and still thrive and be happy!

So yes, entrepreneurship is a calling, and through the inherent value added by the business idea, we can make the world happier while we ourselves become happier.

The problem with entrepreneurship comes with the historical economy's shifting values.

Post–World War, the West created a world where money, fame, and material wealth were the indicators of success. The growing economy and the increase in consumerism led to people working so they could purchase products. Industries mass-produced items, increasing supply and lowering quality.

Unfortunately, we still hold those values nearly eighty years later. The advertising industry targets our hearts and manipulates us into believing we need fancy cars or expensive shoes to be happy. The American "Black Friday" concept has been a hit in our African cities because we've fallen for this extreme consumerism culture. Happier countries like Norway have rejected concepts promoting extreme consumerism and protecting their value systems.

Even our schools further our need for success by making us believe our careers are our number one priority. My physics lecturer at university used to remind us that if we didn't pass, "We will end up like the guys who dig drainage trenches in town." Other similar sayings exist worldwide, such as, "You don't want to end up flipping burgers," which is often heard in the United States.

Let me be clear that there is nothing wrong with motivating others to achieve materially. The problem is the overemphasis on worldly aspects of material and money. This honestly meant a lot to us, as many of my classmates in

Botswana came from villages where money was the key to pulling their families out of poverty.

However, not attending to critical elements of human needs, such as joy, social connection, and a sense of purpose, meant that we believed material success would lead to happiness. On the contrary, work does not have to be dry and soul-sucking!

Every day, in my consulting assignments, I see customers who believe that. The workplace seems largely unchanged despite corporate leaders attending fancy MBA and leadership programs. How is it that after eighty years, we haven't seen the error in our thinking?

People globally acknowledge that work is a key part of their lives. In several studies in Germany, most people rated work as important to their well-being. However, most workers in the US say they do not enjoy their work. When asked, "Do you like what you do each day?" only 20% could give a strong "yes" response.[22]

Imagine how productivity levels could be improved by correcting this mixed-up model. Billions of dollars could be released into the economy as it has been proven that happier workers produce more. Humans have always invested in fun activities—from our African ancestors to Roman games to Indian communities' dancing rituals.

Why is this fun not applied to work?

In Okinawa, Japan, people practice *ikigai*, which comes from *iki,* meaning "to live," and *gai,* meaning "reason." Together, it means "a reason to live." This concept motivates people to live purpose-driven lives that are true to themselves. How appealing does that sound?

Regularly speaking with your team is how you can build relationships that go beyond colleagues. Since its inception, Innolead has always made it part of our values to be open among our team.

We often start meetings with dedicated time for anyone to share a professional or personal highlight. We named it the "I fun moment." It could be something they're looking forward to doing or a recent win at home or at work. As a result, meetings are positive before they even start, and the team feels more connected, allowing for better communication and collaboration.

Take it from me: you can learn a lot about a person based on what they share as a recent highlight, and I've built up a lot of trust with my team.

My hardships have taught me that entrepreneurs need well-defined strategies to support themselves. From start-up pressures to running a sustainable and thriving business, each step of the journey brings its own challenges.

Despite the glamorous perceptions of entrepreneurial life, the way we do it is leaving us sick and even sometimes opening the door to an early grave. Because we are supposed to be tough, gritty, and smart, it is difficult to admit that the occupation has its dark side.

It is estimated that entrepreneurs make up about 5% of the global population, and about 90% of start-ups fail. The odds are stacked against us, especially young people who are most vulnerable. In our part of the world, we have even more red tape in the form of over-regulation, corruption, and lack of infrastructure. However, businesses can still fail anywhere.

According to the World Economic Forum's Global Competitiveness Report, which compares economies worldwide, African countries continue to underperform, especially in key areas like business-friendly policies, innovation, and technology.[23] It is extra hard for entrepreneurs where internet access is either too expensive or has poor bandwidth.

In my journey, I must deal with difficult clients and with lions eating our cattle at our farm. Lions literally eat away at my business! Beyond that, frequent droughts in my area make animal feed expensive. These challenges make it hard to remember the joy of working in nature, but I have to remember that it can't always be perfect.

Management programs I took at the University of Cape Town and Stellenbosch University influenced my early entrepreneurial journey. I also used my knowledge of scenario futuristic planning to plan my business ideas, including assessing my competencies, researching competitive advantages, and analyzing global trends. This led me to consider project management to be an "unmet need" in the market at the time.

As a project engineer at the mines, I had a level of competency I could leverage. The developing industries of Botswana and Africa as a whole meant we could help support the government in infrastructure development. Africa is still way behind with infrastructure development, and this translates into the need for good project management capabilities for efficient implementations.

Applying good practice project management would also assist with combating corruption on capital projects across Africa when proper governance is applied. That is how X-Pert Group and, later, Innolead Consulting were born.

The book *Control Your Destiny, or Someone Else Will* by Noel Tichy and Stratford Sherman taught me the difference innovative leadership can make. I was also inspired by Jim Collins, Peter Drucker, and Henry Mintzberg's business concepts.

In 2015, I joined the Strategic Coach program, one of the best career decisions I have ever made. I was referred by a business friend, James Picknell, who is based in Toronto and had been in Coach for some years, demonstrating the power of networks in business.

Not only was it essential for my life as an entrepreneur, but the holistic nature of the program was phenomenal. I learned to find the balance between work and life, giving me quality time with my friends and family.

Importantly, Coach supported us with tools and processes for running an enterprise and strategies for growth and developing a Self-Managing Company®. The program taught me tools to create time for fun and to apply The 4 Freedoms™ Money, Time, Relationships, and Purpose.

After learning at Strategic Coach about the different freedoms we grant ourselves, I immediately applied the Freedom of Time by declaring Thursday a Free Day™. Throughout my week, this is a priority I set in place to balance my time. Without it, my workaholic tendencies could creep in. They are always knocking in the shadows!

I do nothing related to work on Free Days. I spend time at home or on the farm, and I pursue relaxing and nurturing activities. I've learned it's one thing to say I want to pursue hobbies; it's another actually to prioritize them. The Free Days concept has revolutionized my time management and made fun activities part of my weekly planning. Part of your "Joy" in JoyReP and part of the success formula.

To my pleasant surprise, my team took this well and encouraged me to stay away from the office on Thursdays so I could truly rejuvenate. They even charged me a fee if I appeared in the office, and I had to pay without giving any explanations! The Innolead team is also encouraged to have Free Days, plan for fun, and take leave when there is total dislocation from work.

The Coach program also confirmed the importance of joy and well-being, even for a hyper-competitive entrepreneur like me. It validated my belief that everything we do has to be underlined by some level of fun, purely as a human need that improves well-being and performance.

Such a strategy also allowed my team to join in, loosen up, and start applying the same to their approach to work and life. As a result, our employees are more engaged and productive.

The Coach concept of Unique Ability® (UA) reinforced the need to match one's job occupation to one's superior skills. We sometimes do jobs that bring us down or make us anxious because they are not aligned with our talent makeup.

When you operate in your UA, you both excel in and are passionate about your job, opening the door to flow. Adopting the UA approach maximizes your time on work that matches your superior skills and gives you energy. Innolead and DigitalGae match my knowledge, curiosity, and wisdom signature strengths and allow me to operate in my UA. And the farm connects me with nature and even aspects of spirituality. It's much easier to get into flow.

As more of the team operates in their UA, the business is able to grow 10x in many areas. Work is not a drag, and the business becomes more sustainable in the long term. I experienced this boost of team energy and customer satisfaction. Clients can feel the energy and the enthusiasm to work, which is contagious in itself. It's a normal conversation at Innolead to ensure that team members are operating in their UA as we aim to keep 10xing the business.

I first came across the 10x concept at Coach, and I could relate very well to my journey. Even before joining Coach, I had influenced Innolead to grow 10x in revenue and capabilities. Innolead is now renowned in many industries due to our efficient process of nurturing and growing talent.

One of our past employees, Ms. Lesego Matsheka (now the director at a diamond polishing and cutting company), once said, "My 2-year period at Innolead has been my fastest growth, and I don't think any company can impart such skills on an employee in such record time." Growth is treated as a right in our enterprises.

Once you've made the decision to create value for others, you can start applying 10x to your adventure. *10x Is Easier Than 2x,* co-authored by Benjamin Hardy and Dan Sullivan, defined 10x as "a capability and an operating system one deploys for expansion of your vision, standards, removing non-essentials, developing mastery in unique areas and leading and empowering others who share your vision."

It's about transforming yourself and your teams continuously. You live your life fully, expanding your horizons. You do more with less.

That's how I live my life, combined with the EntreHappiness principles. In this life of abundant opportunities, 10x has never been more doable. With our well-developed infrastructure, educated youth, and peaceful atmosphere, Botswana can embrace 10x growth. In fact, the entire African continent can uplift its economy through entrepreneurship.

Another important part of 10x that Coach encourages is becoming a Self-Managing Company. This way, you, as the CEO, do not have to manage every aspect of day-to-day work. We at Innolead are in the process of making this a reality.

The goal is for the team to focus on operations while the entrepreneur focuses on visionary leadership and new opportunities for the business. You focus more and more on energy-boosting UA areas. Life becomes better and better for the entrepreneur while the business is self-managed by unique teams. This is the "sweet spot" for any entrepreneur, who then can add even more value to society with released time from operations.

I am constantly looking for ways to expand to new areas, like starting my Growth Well podcast, writing this book, speaking at conferences, and creating new products.

Admittedly, I still have to drop in on operations to support my team as we are not yet at full "Self-Managing" status. Identifying who can cover all the areas in management is never easy in Africa, where talent is still in short supply. But with Free Days, I still get to spend more time at the farm and with family, aligning with the joy and relationship parts of JoyReP.

I have met with hundreds of entrepreneurs from early stages to high-achieving millionaires in Africa and America. The common struggles were clear year after year as young men and women struggled to break through the difficult ecosystems and, in the process, tore their lives apart. They lost friends, distanced themselves from family, and missed out on the joys of life. They do this knowing very well that the odds are stacked against them as most start-ups fail.

I won't sugarcoat it; entrepreneurship is difficult. It brings many moments of thrill and despair. Like all jobs, it requires work out of you, but unlike most jobs, much of the pressure is in your hands.

That being said, I don't regret being an entrepreneur. I have come to accept that entrepreneurship is very natural to me. New ventures, curiosity to try new things, and risk-taking are just who I am. If you have the passion and drive, you should kick-start your business idea. You just have to make happiness a priority so you enjoy the ride.

Introducing Happiness

Happiness is a contagious subject. After all, who doesn't want to be happy?

For the past six or so years, I have been following the evolution of happiness in science and books, and as happiness research expands with time, so do my happiness levels. Happiness is an old concept, referring to ancient philosophers over 2,500 years ago. Socrates, Plato, and Aristotle all pondered the subject of what makes a good life and the role of government in facilitating one for its citizens.

Aristotle's work *Nicomachean Ethics* provided an attractive proposition with his concept of happiness, "eudaimonia" or "flourishing." Beyond simply human pleasures, eudaimonia is about achieving life at its most fulfilling point. It is the ultimate goal of human beings.

British philosopher John Locke's concepts of the pursuit of happiness even made it into the American *Declaration of Independence*: "We hold these truths to be self-evident, that all men are created equal, that their Creator endows them with certain unalienable Rights, that among these are Life, Liberty, and pursuit of Happiness."[24] Even governments desire happiness for their citizens.

Despite massive growth in happiness research over recent years, global rates of depression and mental health challenges appear to be getting worse. People are simply not satisfied with their lives because of problems like isolation or lack of success. Entrepreneurs have the added responsibility of trying to launch a business in an economy where so few businesses succeed, and we feel like failures if we cannot provide for our families.

The real turning point in happiness research came with the "positive psychology" movement brought by leaders like Prof. Martin Seligman of the University of Pennsylvania and Dr. Sonja Lyubomirsky of the University of California. Seligman realized that psychology should not only focus on unhappiness and depression but also on how to improve happiness levels. In other words, instead of just raising happiness levels from negative four to negative one, how do we raise them from two to five?

The article "The Benefits of Frequent Positive Affect: Does Happiness Lead to Success?" studies the role of perceived happiness and likability.[25]

Positive affect refers to a person's ability to have positive emotions and an optimistic outlook. Physical signs of this are Duchenne smiles, where a person's cheeks raise when they smile so that wrinkles appear around the eyes. A person with high positive affect will be confident, likable, physically well, and able to cope with stress.

The study looked at photos of women from their senior year of college. Two groups were evaluating the photos: people who knew them at the time of college and those who had never met them.

Both groups perceived that the women with higher positive affect, including Duchenne smiles, were higher in affiliation (generous, considerate, having close relationships) and lower in negative emotions. In addition, the happier women had more successful marriages and relationships.

In her book *The How of Happiness*, Sonja Lyubomirsky created a pie chart to show what determines happiness. Her research shows that 50% is dependent on genetics, 10% on external circumstances (e.g., marriage, place of living), and 40% within the control of the individual.

This means that 40% of your happiness is based on your choices. It can really be an "inside job" where you can dictate your happiness agenda and take charge. If you observe most happy people, they lead purposeful, goal-driven lives.

They take action, whether volunteering in the community, planting trees, starting a business, being active in their garden, learning to play a musical instrument, or climbing Mount Kilimanjaro! They take advantage of this 40% that's in their sphere of influence and up their JoyReP. They don't waste time crying over their circumstance (born in the wrong place!) or blaming their parents for their rather depressive-inclined genes.

I have assessed myself with Sonja Lyubomirsky and Martin Seligman's questionnaires, and, as I mentioned in the previous chapter, I have always scored on the happier side of the scale. My colleagues and team members have always been impressed by my optimism and calm amidst challenges and how I always look at life on the positive side. I am a perpetual optimist and sometimes overly so for my own good.

Admittedly, I have sad, angry, and depressing moments like everyone else. I have learned to study myself, and

I appreciate how I have been able to mitigate unhappy moments. And importantly, we must accept that we all will have unhappy moments occasionally and embrace their role. Unhappiness is not the absence of happiness.

I have especially enjoyed Martin Seligman's PERMA model, which I partly used for the design of the JoyReP formula. I recommend you look into it. It stands for Positive Emotion, Engagement, Relationships, Meaning, and Accomplishments. It looks at well-being holistically, including the pleasures and joys of life.

1. **Positive emotions** capture the feelings of ecstasy, pleasure, love, and warmth.
2. **Engagement**, as we discussed with JoyReP, is how engaged you are in work and how often you are in flow.
3. **Relationships** look at the quality of your relationships with others, including how close you are and how much quality time you spend with others.
4. **Meaning** is your sense of belonging and commitment to something bigger than yourself. This could be family, religion, social causes, business, and politics.
5. **Accomplishments** are the successes you have in work, hobbies, or other areas of your life—a sense of personal mastery.

Seligman has turned PERMA into a measuring tool people can use to assess themselves and work on improvements. He also evolved the model into Positive Education for schools, which we talked about in Chapter One when Marty and I tried to bring it to Botswana. The PERMA model even formed part of the development of the JoyReP formula.

There are various surveys and questionnaires you can use to measure your happiness levels and evaluate your baseline happiness. I recommend Martin Selligman's VIA

Classification of Character Strengths and Virtues and Sonja Lyubomirsky's Subjective Happiness Scale. All are accessible on the Internet.[26] [27]

Happiness is so much more than how many trophies you have or how big your house is. True joy comes from internal fulfillment and a positive mindset. It's the best investment you can make for yourself, so start.

Happiness, African Style

Before we move on to EntreHappiness, let me comment further on the African context I grew up in and how I have seen happiness in my life.

I have many fond memories of warmth, gratitude, and achievements in my African upbringing. I can vividly recall how we used to play games outside (*ko patlelong* or "in the open dirt") in the village and towns with cousins and neighbors. We would run in the rain, spinning around (a game called *mmampudulele*) enjoying the smell as it hit the dry earth.

As a young boy in Gaborone, I played soccer almost daily in the streets after school. We played with marbles, yo-yos, and even empty tires, racing and rolling them. We had competitions jumping over fences across yards.

Chinese movies dominated our movie screens, and we would engage in fights, imitating Bruce Lee or one of the funny characters in *Half a Loaf of Kung Fu*. This was all before the social media era, which kept children from playing outside, having fun, and making friends.

Despite my mother's challenges of bringing up four kids, she would sometimes dance for us. There was a dance called "bump jive" then, and we would dance together to the beat of the music.

Late every afternoon, Mma Mmiga walked over five kilometers from the school with a bunch of school books in one hand and a plastic bag with goodies from the store in the other hand. I remember the feeling of warmth as I watched her walk toward our house cheerily. She would shout out, "Mike, please prepare a nice cup of tea for me!" We looked forward to the fresh loaf of bread she brought as I lit up the paraffin stove and put on the kettle.

Growing up in the village and on the streets of Gaborone, we were happy in my book! We had nothing to compare life with, and our world was the best despite not having the Western style. Like the San tribes in the Kgalagadi desert of Botswana, lack of material wealth does not have to translate to misery and unhappiness. Even the native people of America lived a much more psychologically pleasing and happier life before the settlers landed, bringing material competition and breaking the social fabric.

These childhood memories are permanent reminders of the simple happiness of childhood: playing with friends, dancing with my mother, and finding joy in a loaf of bread handmade by Mma Mmiga on the coal stove. I sometimes have these Proust moments, a moment named after writer Marcel Proust where there is a sudden involuntary and intense remembering, the past promptly emerging from a smell, taste, or texture.

The older I get, the more I realize there are moments of happiness all around me if I only recognize them for what they are. Just staring at the sky, stargazing at our farm on a dead, quiet dark night, can bring the soul an overwhelming feeling of calmness and warmth. Playing with and petting our two rottweiler dogs can boost my mood for the day. You don't need lots of money to bring happiness home.

According to Maslow's Hierarchy of Needs, happiness is achieved at the final stage of self-actualization. This means that it would be harder for the developing world to find happiness because the lower levels of the hierarchy, physiological needs, and safety are not as widely satisfied. I do not strictly subscribe to this thought, as happiness is a choice irrespective of your economic situation.

That doesn't mean it's impossible to lack food or shelter and be happy, but it makes it much harder. It is possible, as exemplified by ancient tribes across the world. For this reason, the developed Western world is able to focus on happiness more than Africa and other continents, where poverty and conflict are still entrenched.

The UN has also recognized the importance of well-being with the declaration in 2012 of the annual UN World Happiness Report. In this, it is clear that happiness is far from the mainstream for developing countries like Botswana, where despite major strides in development, the focus is still primarily based on eradicating poverty and building a middle-class economy.

In 2018, I presented at a Botswana budget conference on "National Budgeting for Happiness," and it was clear from the reception that this was a very infantish idea to policymakers and the public at large.

Strangely, Botswana and other African countries continue to underperform in terms of well-being ranking, and one would have thought some level of urgency would be required. My desire is for Botswana and other African countries to appreciate the role of happiness in development and that it is not a luxury but a desire by all people on earth, irrespective of economic status.

Governments around the world have established ministries and departments responsible for happiness, such as Dubai and the small country of Bhutan, which has popularized the application of the Gross Happiness Index versus GDP as a key measure of well-being. As the experts say, when one's annual salary gets to $70,000, no additional amounts would result in an additional happiness level.

It is a pity that our countries are losing the essence of African values that sustained a certain level of well-being and happiness, albeit in a survival state. Relationships, celebrations, rituals, and dancing marinate joy and play. The San, an indigenous African group, would dance around a fire at night with family and friends after a day of hunting.

In Botswana, the start of the planting season is still celebrated, led by the chief, with villagers congregating at the Kgotla to celebrate together. The Kgotla is the court or the meeting place for the chief and his people's consultation and where villages will meet for celebration.

Industrialization comes in and steals the playful side of our lives. The developed countries, especially the Scandinavian countries, continue to dominate the top happiest countries in the world with their highly pro-people policies and strong economies.

Although I agree with Maslow's hierarchy in some regards, I do not believe it is as clear as it seems. It is definitely true that developing countries find it harder to be happy because they lack security; however, we can also see that a sense of happiness can exist with the right mindset. Unhealthy comparisons are the ones that lead to unhappiness and divisiveness as we compete to look like and emulate Western cultures.

Even if a person does not have a lot in a material sense, they can still find the four parts of JoyReP, though they should not stop striving for higher levels of needs.

Introducing EntreHappiness

Entrepreneurs are at the heart of human development through the technologies they bring and their ideas that improve the standard of living. Entrepreneurs like Bill Gates, Richard Branson, Mark Zuckerberg, and Larry Page operate tirelessly off the radar and have made the world better.

Regardless of their importance in the world, entrepreneurs still face daunting challenges, as we'll discuss more in Chapter Eight. As a result, families break up, alcoholism can set in, diseases can take over our bodies, and suicidal thoughts can invade our minds.

This is why I came up with EntreHappiness: to encourage struggling entrepreneurs who can't find the way to freedom. I know what that's like.

As an entrepreneur in my 30s and 40s, I faced burnout and some levels of depression. Unaware of the science of joy and happiness, I started to apply techniques that ensured high energy levels and made me ready to address conflict (which normally brought me anxiety) and the challenges of running a business.

It was never easy, but the effects were evident. I exercised, read, maintained close connections with my family, and ate increasingly nutritious foods (thanks to my wife, Nancy!). Eating green smoothies, bone broths, and traditional Tswana wholesome foods is common in our house.

Fun also characterized my life. Nancy loves cooking and hosting friends as one of our fun activities. We would have a bountiful amount of tasty dishes, listen to music, dance our hearts out, and blow the music volume. There's nothing like a joyous time with friends! My wife and I have always loved music and relaxing together while listening to old tunes.

My love for my kids and wanting what's best for them influenced my purpose in life. Visiting my mum with Nancy over weekends and having tea always brought me joy, even more so when my siblings and their partners joined.

My friends were also nearby when I needed light moments over a drink. Like me, one of my friends is a runner, and we would participate in marathon runs and always push for twenty-one-kilometer runs, which we would complete. My weekly runs also contribute to good, healthy, and happier days. These social connections and physical exercise are vital for being a happy entrepreneur.

These strategies I naturally applied are how entrepreneurship connects to happiness, thus EntreHappiness.

A 1994 study of 272 employees over the course of eighteen months revealed the impact of positive emotions in the workplace.[28] Those who were more positive had enhanced performance, improved relationships, increased job satisfaction, and stress reduction. Overall, they performed better and were healthier people.

Tony Robbins interviewed billionaires in the US and found that only a minority appeared happy. We say if we had more money, then we would be truly happy.[29] But the wealthiest people are not happy. I trust that by now, the point has been drilled home.

If not money, then what?

To endure the challenges of entrepreneurs, the art of happiness must become an integral part of entrepreneurial development. Not only does it help with stress and anxiety, but it also improves productivity levels and allows them to thrive physically, mentally, and spiritually. Applying these strategies can also add to a longer, healthier, and happier lifespan.

Once you start to apply these strategies, it's important to stop and think about how well they are or are not working. If something isn't working for you, it's okay to change it. What's best for me is not going to be good for everyone, and that's alright!

I have devised eight key components for entrepreneurial happiness. That's not to say that these are the only ways to be happy, but they are certainly a start. Many of them also incorporate your life outside of work, so always be looking at how work or personal life changes how you apply them.

First, before we get into those keys, let's talk about grit, endurance, and resilience. We have discussed all three of those concepts already, and they are vital for happiness.

As I described in Chapter Four, grit is the ability to remain dedicated to long-term goals despite obstacles. If you let challenges bring you down, you won't find true happiness. Instead, we endure, which means facing the situation without giving in to it, and then being resilient by bouncing back when the challenge is over.

You can also see the aspects of JoyReP in EntreHappiness. Joy, Relationships, Engagement, and Purpose will always be important, no matter the situation.

Now, let's jump into the components of happiness. There may be some that are easy for you, while others may seem impossible. Focus on them one at a time if you have to, but don't assume that you aren't able to do something. Resilience and grit are about pushing yourself, not about giving up because something seems hard or causes doubt.

Trust me, these eight EntreHappiness Keys make all the difference. They have done it for me and millions across the world, and now it's your turn!

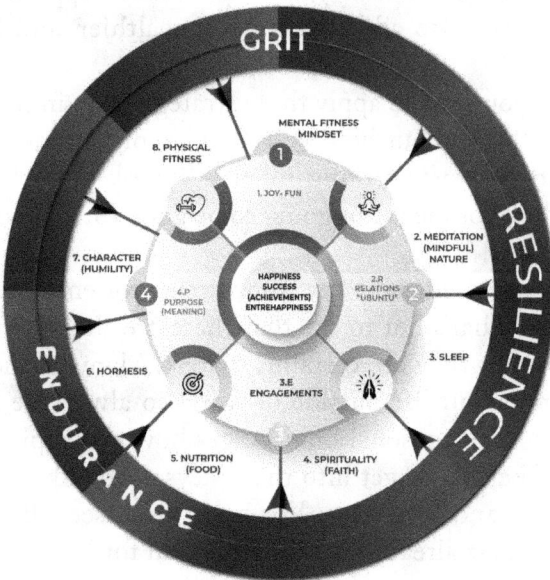

The Eight Keys

1. Mental Fitness Mindset

Mental fitness refers to the well-being of our mental and cognitive functions. It relates to our mental agility, how fast we think or adapt to changes, and to our mindfulness, how aware we are of our own thoughts and feelings.

It is very common for entrepreneurs and people in general to say that we have to exercise our bodies, but we rarely focus on emotional or mental fitness.

We can improve our mental fitness by stimulating our brains with puzzles, reading, and learning new skills. Other things we will talk about, like exercise and sleep, will also help keep your mind operating at full capacity. Self-care, meditation, and stress management can help return your center to the present moment and ensure that your mind is clear from distractions.

I have pursued new activities, such as learning guitar and starting a podcast, so I can keep my mind sharp. My house is full of debates (with our kids) about anything from Trump and Carl Jung to Marxism. My wife is a lawyer, so she is a practiced debater. These discussions keep us thinking in new ways and sharpening our existing ideas.

This is also one reason why I chose a profession based on intellectual know-how: management consulting. First, as an engineer and now as a consultant, I have ways to use my knowledge and wisdom. New challenges keep me thinking on my feet, and I have to be at my best when dealing with clients, hence continuous reading and researching.

I have seen firsthand the negative effects of not prioritizing mental fitness. My mother was a bright lady, but when she retired, she didn't do anything to keep her brain active. Eventually, dementia set in, and she deteriorated mentally until she passed.

I feel I lost a loved one because she "retired" and did not understand the importance of mental fitness to keep her cognitive abilities alive. For this reason, I no longer believe in the principle of retirement and rather believe we should rewire our brains for new meaning or purpose.

On the other hand, I did a podcast with an elderly man who is an environmental activist in Botswana, and I believe he will age slower because he fills his life with activities that keep him mentally sharp. He achieved a doctorate degree in his 70s, and he is a columnist for a weekly newspaper. No retirement, I say!

Positive self-talk is one way you can clear your mind when you're facing a stressful situation. You might find your mind filled with doubts and worries, but take those thoughts and turn them around to be encouraging for yourself.

Instead of "I don't know how to handle this," try "I can figure this out." Instead of "I'm not cut out for this," think, "I am just as capable as anyone else."

The more you train your brain to stop those negative thoughts and turn them positive, the more naturally an optimistic mindset will come. Soon, you will do it without even thinking about it.

You can also learn a new language, do puzzles or brain teasers, and journal. When you feel your brain working, you'll know you're keeping it active.

Entrepreneurship, in a true sense, should be a "calling" and therefore should have no room for retiring but doing more and more of what you love. That way, you continue making contributions to society while you stay mentally sharp, and you are sure to live longer!

2. Meditation and Nature

Both my maternal and paternal lines were active in agriculture; my grandfather loved his cattle, and my mother was into orchards and plants. Those memories stayed with me, and by my fortieth birthday, I had acquired a farm for livestock. Calm, close-to-nature farming activities balanced the hyper-competitive, energy-draining, city-based consulting.

Of course, farming is not for the faint of heart, as there are still cash flow issues and droughts. But overall, I have loved the mix of consulting, technology, and farming. I try to hack the systems so they work "my way," as the more they are "my way," the more fun I have.

There is nothing like watching happy cows jump amidst beautiful green pastures with colorful butterflies and bird songs in the nearby acacia trees. It's a symphony that is hard to describe, and it really makes me feel one with nature! Taking walks on the farm to check the quality of grazing, I would enjoy the sight of the different tree types, including the majestic camelthorn tree and the strong shepherd tree parading the bushes.

Even as you apply all these strategies, stress is inevitable. There will be unforeseen and overwhelming challenges in your business and personal lives. Even if you have back-to-back deadlines, you can take a few minutes to meditate and calm your mind. Close your eyes and focus on the physical space around you. If you are spiritual like me, you can say a word of gratitude or prayer.

If you recall from Chapter Two, my grandfather meditated before meditation was even popularized. He would sit by the tree, still and relaxed. Now, we have scientific proof that meditation lowers stress, clears a busy mind, and increases self-awareness. Meditation is not, by any means, a new concept.

Beginners can meditate by finding meditation apps or recorded meditations on sites such as YouTube. You won't be able to stop yourself from thinking, but you can acknowledge your thoughts and then let them pass.

Focus on your muscles and your body, feeling your feet against the floor or your back against a chair. Breathe slowly, and make sure you have a quiet and comfortable environment.

I combine my love of nature with the importance of meditation. My farm is one of the quietest places I can go, and it has very few distractions. Many evenings, I will sit by the fire and look up at the stars as I meditate.

Meditating can take as little or as much time as you want it to. If you only have five minutes before your next meeting, do some basic breathing and thought exercises. If you have a couple of hours to yourself in the evening, try something longer. Work it around your schedule as much as you can.

As long as you are consistently meditating, you will notice a difference. It took me years to appreciate the value of meditation, and doing yoga classes helped a lot.

3. Sleep

Sleep is incredibly important. It supports the immune system, lowers stress, improves memory, and contributes to a longer lifespan. It's the time when long-term memories are encoded and consolidated. The brain clears out waste, and your body repairs itself.

So why do entrepreneurs think we can be successful on little sleep?

At the start of Innolead, I thought this, too. I saw the rockstar entrepreneurs who didn't sleep and tried to emulate that. Now, as a 55-year-old, I see how poor sleep as a young adult hurts my current health, and I often have to remind my son that getting only 4 hours of sleep is not a badge of honor!

It can be easy to think that time sleeping is time wasted because you could be working on your business, but a good night's sleep is going to set you up for a fresh day better than a restless night.

According to Mark Hyman's article "8 Simple Hacks for a Better Night's Sleep," a study found that even a partial night's sleep increases insulin resistance, which can lead to diabetes.[30] Hyman says that in order to get better sleep, you should get on a regular routine, get regular sun exposure, and turn off electronics one or two hours before bed. Yes, you got it: switch off your smartphone two hours before bed.

I get my best sleep when I go to the farm. Like I already described, it's dark and dead quiet, unlike in the city. The night will be disturbed by the occasional howling of jackals in the distance and the roosters crowing early morning, signaling the start of the day.

Without distractions like phones or TV, I will fall asleep as I meditate by the fire, and in order to not disturb my sleep, I'll crawl right into bed without even brushing my teeth (only when Nancy is not there)!

When I wake up after a night on the farm, I am ready to embrace the day. It is a feeling, unlike the one in the city where there is both noise and light pollution at night. Waking up close to nature, I feel refreshed, full of creativity and energy. I get my best creative work done there.

This is also why my wife and I live just outside of the city and in a semi-farming area. It's next to a nature reserve, and we enjoy birds, indigenous trees, the sounds and sights of nature, beautiful sunsets, and an overall calm environment.

I feel at peace in a way I couldn't if we lived within the city, and it contributes to our overall well-being as a family. Anxiety is sure to be the enemy of sleep, and for entrepreneurs, wandering minds can be a problem. Entrepreneurs get hit with bad news at any time, sometimes early at night before going to bed.

The finance manager can say, "We don't have adequate funds to pay all the salaries!" And then my brain goes into overdrive. These then trigger anxiety and destroy any chances of deep sleep.

So, I try to avoid anxiety triggers at least two hours before bed. I stay away from my emails, don't take calls that I suspect could raise my blood pressure, avoid watching crisis news on TV, and stay away from the phone an hour before bed.

During my days of workaholism, I used to sleep an average of six to seven hours, which means a small amount of deep sleep. For the past few years, I have done my best to get off the phone an hour before sleep (never easy!) so I can get to bed by 10 p.m. (which means sound asleep by 10:30) and wake up by 6:30, giving me a healthy dose of eight hours of sleep.

I have seen a huge difference as my illness frequency has decreased, and even if I have a cold, it has never been intense for many years. The other EntreHappiness Keys also contribute to improved immunity, such as regular exercise, hormesis, and eating right.

4. Spirituality and Faith

Spiritual entrepreneurship has always been part of my inner game. The creativity of identifying unmet needs, the urge to serve, and the joy of working with others toward a common purpose represent a higher calling.

I believe in a connection between the universe and all living things. We should have endless love for others and for nature. Spirituality is the urge that keeps us going despite roadblocks. Our purpose becomes greater than ourselves. It's not about money or popularity but love for others and connection to the universe.

To me, spirituality is the feeling I got when the Innolead team delivered a technology conference called i-Connect for the second time, resulting in over 300 delegates and raving feedback.

It's in securing global speakers like Salim Ismail and John Kamara to our conferences as it is never easy due to their hectic schedules.

It's when farm workers acknowledge and are openly thankful for how much we've impacted their lives with the empowerment approach and the respect we show. It is a whole social transformation for them when they have improved housing, electricity from solar, and even television for the first time.

It's the feeling I get when walking through the bushveld at the farm and listening to the rhythm of my boots as they brush against the nutritious grasses that our livestock live on. I get awash with magical, transcendental feelings as I experience a connection with the universe and feel there is something bigger out there.

Spirituality, in this sense, does not directly mean religion. In a study, Dr. Kenneth Kendler found that personal devotion and personal conservatism go hand in hand for some people but not all.[31]

This is important because we see many people who strictly adhere to religious rules but don't necessarily live them out in their daily lives. Dr. Kendler also found three correlations between spirituality and mental health:

1. Lower likelihood of depression
2. Buffer against challenges (e.g., illness and loss of a loved one)
3. Lower likelihood of becoming an addict

I am not advocating for any specific religion or lack thereof. Spirituality will look different in each person based on their morals and beliefs.

I was brought up Catholic. I went through confirmation and served as an altar boy. Even as a young boy, I prayed every day before bedtime as taught by the scriptures. This idea of gratitude added humility to my life.

Despite my upbringing as a Catholic, my bias toward sciences and engineering education brought me to question religious practices in the traditional sense. This is very common now with many young people who struggle to make sense of the God that talked to people in the Old Testament and that God is watching us all the time. The concept of the Big Bang and scientific explanations started to appeal to me.

My mother, a staunch Christian, was not happy when I started to doubt religion, but it was a natural process I went through as I thought about what I believed instead of only following what was in the scriptures or what she told me.

As I entered the entrepreneurial world, I carried that underlying spirituality. I evolved to believe there is something bigger out there, an ideology called pantheism.

I look out at nature and can't help but believe that with all the intricacies, something created all of it. An intelligent system started everything. Baruch Spinoza discussed this universal God. Pantheism's main ideas involve a God who is synonymous with the universe. It created the world, but it does not concern itself with people. Einstein stated, "I believe in Spinoza's God," which many take to mean even he was a pantheist.

Whatever faith principle you choose, it is a proven fact that having some sort of spiritual faith is beneficial to well-being. The Blue Zones are areas across the world that are seen as particularly happy and healthy. People often live longer and healthier lives based on nine common factors that researchers have noted.

One such factor is spirituality. According to the Blue Zones website, "All but five of the 263 centenarians we interviewed belonged to some faith-based community ... Research shows that attending faith-based services four times per month will add 4-14 years of life expectancy."

The denomination doesn't matter if you keep your mind open to something bigger than yourself. For me, I experience spirituality through nature, as in Spinoza and Einstein.

A game changer for me has been the book *The Spirituality of Imperfection* by Ernest Kurtz and Katherine Ketcham. As they say in the book, we are incapable of finding all the answers, and our peace only comes when we accept that.

When the 2008 recession hit our business, and we had to retrench close to half our staff, I wondered why.

When we lost tenders to companies from outside the country, and our brilliant young employees needed such projects and had to be retrenched, I wondered.

When my son Motheo was troubled by a rare hip condition that led to over nine surgery operations, I wondered.

When I observed my mother deteriorate over a ten-year period due to dementia, I wondered.

But at the same time, when I lived through my healthiest periods in my 30s and 40s, I also wondered.

I wondered when Innolead made profits year on year for over ten years.

When I got to join the prestigious Strategic Coach program through referrals, I wondered.

It's a mix of good and bad, and that's just how it is. The true spirituality of imperfection.

I don't want to romanticize suffering, but it has become clear that it is part of the human formula. I believe that we have to be prepared for suffering, especially as entrepreneurs in a challenging climate, and spirituality is one way to give us a foundation to deal with these inevitable challenges.

We in Africa are often spiritual people. Many of our religions are influenced by the West because of missionaries, but we have our own spiritual practices as well, based on ancestral spirits. Spirituality is inherent in most African tribes.

One of the entrepreneurs I admire in Botswana is Mompoloki Mogobe, a self-made real estate magnate who has become a friend of mine. I have been on his Mogobe Nuggets podcast, while he has been on my Growth Well podcast, sharing entrepreneurial experiences and insights.

He is a Seventh-Day Adventist faith follower, and when talking to him, I can detect his calmness and clarity of mind that comes from his faith in God. He has overcome emotional scars that he withstood only by believing in something greater than himself.

Entrepreneurs need to believe in something that can support the weight of their struggles. If we don't believe in some higher purpose or power, we will be crushed when difficulties come.

5. Nutrition

You would be amazed to realize how much your diet affects your well-being and overall performance.

Foods high in sugar and carbohydrates can cause energy spikes and crashes, leaving you more drained. Meals balanced with protein and healthy fat give you more sustained energy. There may be specific vitamins or electrolytes that your body naturally lacks, but vitamin-rich food or supplements can balance them.

Individual foods can also have different impacts depending on the quantity. Americans celebrating Thanksgiving know that a turkey dinner can make you feel tired, but in moderation, it can also have a calming effect if you're stressed.

With so many unexpected effects of food, it's no wonder a single meal can change how we feel the rest of the day. And the precise impacts vary per person. Allergies or intolerance can affect the consequences of eating, and even food preferences can alter your mood.

As you look at your diet, ensure you balance protein, fruits and vegetables, grains, and dairy. That does not mean you can't live well on an unbalanced diet (as I often did, eating mainly porridge growing up), but if you can afford to vary your diet, do so.

You should also drink plenty of water and remember that even sugar like chocolate can be good for you in moderation. Think of how your favorite sweet treat is a mood booster!

Another proven example of nutrition's power is found in the Blue Zones. Of the nine different factors for people of this long lifespan, three of them are about diet. They live on what has been now termed the "Mediterranean diet," which is rich in fibre (plant-based) and protein.

First, they eat fewer portions and are known to eat until they are 80% full, not 100%. If you are unaware of what this feels like, it may be hard initially to get used to this idea. It's all about intuition and listening to your body.

Don't wait until you feel full or like you can't eat another bite. You shouldn't feel hungry but rather comfortable and energized. Overeating can make you low on energy.

The second factor is eating a mainly plant-based diet. People in these areas typically ate meat less than five times a month! When they did eat meat, they chose pork or fish.

Otherwise, they ate vegetables, legumes (such as beans or lentils), and foods high in fiber. They avoided artificial sweeteners and got fat from natural sources like olive oil or nuts. They consumed dairy in moderation.

To some people, this diet might sound similar to what they already do, but to other people, this could sound torturous. I get it; you may not want to give up meat or processed foods. As I mentioned, I love cheesecake and chocolate and get more enjoyment out of eating those.

That being said, you can still apply this diet occasionally.

If you eat meat more than once a day, try cutting back to once or even only a few times per week and see what happens. In most parts of Southern Africa, which has a history of cattle farming, meat eating is a long entrenched practice that is difficult to shake off. However, reducing red meat consumption is known to have excellent health benefits.

I have cut my red meat intake to three times a week and replaced it with beans as my protein source. The rest I take from fish and chicken. One of the things that made me very unpopular with our kids was the "no meat day" policy that we had in our house. The idea was to educate our kids to appreciate that there are other, healthier alternatives to red meat, such as beans.

Use olive oil instead of butter when cooking, and generally back off on dairy.

The more often you incorporate this diet, the better for your body, but if you try something for a while and end up unhappy because you miss certain foods, it's not cheating to indulge occasionally.

The last factor is to drink alcohol in moderation.

A few Blue Zones didn't drink at all, but many were more than happy to drink as long as it wasn't in excess. Moderate drinkers tended to outlive non-drinkers.

That doesn't mean you should be encouraged to grab a bar for shots every night. People typically drank one or two glasses, often red wine. The Blue Zones website specifies that you can't "save up" your drinks to splurge one day a week.

In the end, it's up to you if you want to drink or not. As I said, some of the Blue Zones didn't drink at all, often due to religious reasons. But don't think that alcohol is bad for you. As long as it's in moderation, it can have surprising benefits.

The more attention you pay to your diet, the better benefits you will have. If you often feel sick or bloated, you can cut out one food group at a time until you find out what the issue is.

You should also note what energizes you and try to avoid mindless snacking. Eat because you're hungry, not because it tastes good.

As Africans, we have the traditional wholesome foods that our ancestors ate. As hunters and gatherers, we lived on wild fruits and meat from wild animals. Our modern high starch and sugar foods did not exist. Sugar was a treat of wild berries or the occasional beehive find.

Today, the average American eats twenty-two teaspoons of sugar a day! Unfortunately, we have copied the American high-processed foods culture, leading to a runaway rise in non-communicable diseases such as hypertension and type 2 diabetes.

Certain food cravings can also clue you into what vitamins you may be lacking. For example, craving red meat could mean you're low on iron, and craving sugar or chocolate could mean you need magnesium or water.

As an entrepreneur with a desire for longevity and vitality throughout your career, I encourage you to change your diet closer to the African-style free-range meats and the Mediterranean diet. And immediately cut your sugar intake!

Try changing your diet to see what works for you, then stick with it.

6. Hormesis

Hormesis is the process of exposing yourself to low doses of potentially harmful substances or stressors. For example, most people would agree that exercise is good for your body, but it is definitely possible to overdo it.

An older person who is not in shape should not go out and run a marathon without any training, but a short jog or walk coupled with basic stretches is good for anyone. This is evidenced when a person is sore after a workout. The body rebuilds muscles to be stronger, which causes pain but is ultimately good.

Earlier in the book, I used the analogy of metal hardening as it is processed. It becomes tougher when you use a mallet hammer.

Man is made of the same material. When stressed, the body responds by becoming more substantial and more resilient.

Dr. Mark Hyman, a hormetic expert, recommends many hormetic strategies:

- Time-restricted eating and fasting (I have been practicing intermittent fasting for the past five years)
- High-intensity interval training and strength training
- Cold plunges and saunas
- Breathwork, hypoxia (low oxygen states)
- Hyperbaric oxygen therapy
- Ozone therapy
- Light therapy
- Phytochemicals[32]

According to Dr. Hyman, these strategies produce effects by turning on a series of healing systems that activate DNA repair, cool off inflammation, increase your body's antioxidant systems, stimulate stem cell production, increase neuroplasticity, and increase insulin sensitivity.

Exercise has proven to be one of the most effective ways of staying healthy. I have already described my history of athleticism, which has helped me stay active. I do weekly jogging and fifteen minutes of stretching and strength exercises in the mornings. This has kept me in shape and able to cope with daily stresses. You can walk, do yoga, or do aerobics.

I have been extremely lucky that hyperbaric oxygen therapy is available in Botswana. This type of treatment involves breathing pure oxygen inside a specialized chamber. I have been using it for the past twelve months as part of my cancer treatment protocol, but it can be used by anyone for health benefits safely.

Another example is cold showers, something I have incorporated into my life. Extreme sports athletes would spend hours swimming in the icy waters of Antarctica, but for ordinary folks, a short cold shower is proven to relieve pain, improve circulation, and boost mood.

I start my mornings with cold showers. As Mark Harper says, a cold shower in the morning is like drinking a cup of coffee. The cold water results in a dopamine rush, and you can feel alive for a few hours after the exposure. Some people even do ice baths, but that's not for me. It took me three years to get used to cold showers! There is no competition, so you can take your time, and once used to it, it becomes a lifetime practice that adds to your well-being and longevity.

Other uses of hormesis include short fasts, moderate alcohol intake, heat exposure like saunas, and certain foods with small amounts of toxins, like caffeine or garlic.

I look at nature and wonder why we ever thought we needed three meals a day. Lions can go weeks without eating. Growing up, we would wake up early and not eat until midday, and then we adopted the Western culture of three meals that, in my view, has resulted in the current obesity problems in our societies.

Dr. David Sinclair, Harvard Medical School professor of genetics and expert on aging, says we should eat less often.[33] He only eats one main meal a day, with light snacking in between. For breakfast, David will drink coffee, tea, or water, but no food. As a result, he says he has more energy and feels better. According to him, intermittent fasting has provided the best weight control for his body. I can attest to that since starting fasting seven years ago, my ideal weight has been consistent.

My wife inspired me to eat healthier and fast. The longest she has fasted is twenty-one days (as part of diabetes treatment). The most I have done is three days. For a while, I fasted every Tuesday and only drank water. But after some years, I changed to the sixteen-hour fast where I eat a late breakfast around 11 a.m. and then eat my main meal for supper around 6 p.m. This has worked for me, and my body system has now fully adjusted to this routine. Two meals a day now for over three years.

The science of fasting is fascinating. Your body switches from burning sugar to fat, which is optimal for weight loss. The body cleans out damaged cells, a process called autophagy. This is believed to protect against aging, disease, and inflammation. After a few days, your body will work harder to conserve protein. It literally prepares itself to go longer without food.

Fasting does not have to look like going without food for a full 24 hours. You can also do 18:6, where you only eat for a six-hour period, or choose any variation that fits your schedule. There is no one best way to fast.

My wife and I love spending time in a dry sauna–another form of hormesis. We regularly do twenty-five minutes twice a week. Both dry and wet saunas improve respiratory health, detox the body through sweat, and relax muscles. Too much heat can be dangerous, but this amount is enough to make us stronger.

The concept of hormesis asserts that small amounts of stress can promote longevity. The more tolerant your body is to some of these stressors, like exercise, the more you can increase the amount of stress. However, other stressors, like heat exposure, should always be limited.

As you expose your body to low amounts of stress, you allow your body to build back stronger than before. Like a callus, your body repairs itself in a way that sets it up to withstand even more next time. Talk about biohacking for well-being and longevity!

I do a combination of physical exercise, cold morning showers, hyperbaric oxygen, dry sauna, and intermittent fasting. It took a few years to get the rhythm. Some of these are pretty pricey, like hyperbaric oxygen therapy, and also not as accessible as saunas. But exercise, fasting, and cold showers are well within your control, so let's get going!

7. Character (Humility)

Everyone has values. They may be different for each person and even within families, but everyone has a set of morals they live by. For example, my siblings are all different in personality, but we have inherited good manners from our mother and community.

Understanding your virtues and strengths is essential. Philosophers like Aristotle believed a life of virtue leads to happiness. Studies from religion and philosophy have culminated in a summary of six virtues that can assess their top strengths, as researched by Martin Seligman with his VIA Character Strengths.

The six virtues are:

1. Humanity
2. Wisdom and Knowledge
3. Courage
4. Temperance
5. Transcendence
6. Justice

The first thing I look for in people to work with is character. I want to see how they treat other people and if they follow through with what they start.

I bring this idea to Innolead every day. First, I keep myself in check. I want to set a good example for our employees and my colleagues. I can't expect anyone to have good character if I don't. Clients often give the job to the people whose character they like. They need to know they can rely on you.

I have always kept character a priority in our recruitment. A candidate's technical competencies come second to character. Character and values are the most important elements for good, healthy relationships. It pleases me to hear clients praise my team for their character because I know I can count on them, and trust is the backrock of any organization.

My team knows they need to keep their promises. They should take ownership and explain the situation if they unexpectedly can't. As a result, my team is likable and trustworthy.

Botswana's economy is going through a tough time as lab-grown diamonds are hurting the market for natural diamonds. The economy is suffering, and Innolead and DigitalGae have been hit hard. We had to apply retrenchment processes to optimize cash flows.

It has been a very emotionally tough time for me as we had to part with team members who have been with us for over ten years! We developed close relationships and have truly become like a family.

However, my biggest source of support has been from my current partners, Chilipi Mogasha and Okitanye Gaogane. We have worked as a team to resolve the situation, and our close relationship, which has been built over fifteen years, has helped us.

As a result, the experience has become less daunting, and we are navigating the difficult times confidently. We remind ourselves that we should not waste a "good crisis" and remain optimistic about what we extract from the difficult times.

There have been times I have been impressed by a person's character, and there are other times I have been thoroughly disappointed. Years ago, way before the 2016 American election, I read one of Donald Trump's books, *Think Big and Kick Ass: In Business and Life*. I remember there was a chapter where he talked about how someone messed him up, and he wouldn't let that pass. In other words, he was going to square up and go after that person! I thought to myself, "Why am I reading this book?"

He was a super entrepreneur who was incredibly successful and knowledgeable on the subject. But I couldn't get past the fact that he was going after people who let him down, even after just one mistake. People mess up; it's a part of life. By no means has he ever made an error.

I thought to myself that this was not a good guy, even back then, before he was really in the news. He was playing a boyish ego game. And these books end up contaminating our aspiring youths who think such behavior is acceptable as an entrepreneur.

I learned quickly that if I had the choice between dinner with Donald Trump or someone else, I would not choose Trump. Some people would, and that's okay, but he did not align with my morals. You have to be clear about who you're associating with.

Another part of having good character is humility. You may be knowledgeable or have bright ideas, but you are not the only one. You are no better or worse than anyone else. As I talked about spirituality, one thing that can help is practicing gratitude. Whether making a mental note or writing a list down, keep track of what you are grateful for. The more often you do it, the more in control and optimistic you will be.

As illogical as it may sound, you can even be grateful for the challenges you face, imagining the good that may come from them. For example, securing funding for your business can make you more outgoing and passionate. Sometimes, the only benefit you see might be that the nightmare will be over, and that's okay, too!

Other ways to build good character are to be honest, practice empathy, own up to mistakes, keep a positive attitude, and support others.

Author David Brooks talks about two virtues: the resumé virtue and the eulogy virtue. It is the latter we don't usually talk about, yet it quickly unveils at someone's funeral.[34] There, we refer to the deceased as a father and husband. David is very correct. We should first be known for our eulogy virtue: a husband, a brother, and an uncle! Not by our position at work or as some rockstar entrepreneur. Those resumé virtues should not be your prime identity.

Character has worked for me throughout my career. I only associate with people who are first aligned with my values system, whether staff, customers, suppliers, friends, or even family members. I have cut ties with family members who had an unattractive value system, and we have parted with employees who failed to meet our character expectations.

Importantly, good character builds a business with a good character, which can translate to business growth. Clients love dealing with good character souls; even if you have superior technical skills, deals can be lost over arrogance, or rudeness, or not finishing what you start.

Good character traits lead to referability, and we've seen plenty of that in our business, where we have been invited to take on opportunities purely due to our reliability and general good habits. It can build your brand and bring in new business.

Character as a whole is a broad concept, but it is important. You will foster personal growth and build more meaningful relationships with others if you have clear morals and a strong character.

8. Physical Fitness

Regular exercise is essential no matter your age. According to experts, it works on your body's biological systems. It builds endurance, releases built-up energy, enhances immune function, and improves mental health.[35]

The Mayo Clinic reports that exercise can prevent and lower the risk of death from stroke, metabolic syndrome, high blood pressure, type 2 diabetes, depression, cancer, arthritis, and even falls![36] Another study showed that dementia risk was nearly twice as high for the less fit compared to the more fit.[37]

Since I joined the Botswana Junior Tennis Club in secondary school, I have seen the importance of regular physical activity. After a rough day, a five-mile jog can do wonders in letting off steam and freeing my mind.

Not everyone likes to climb a flight of stairs, let alone run several miles. You can exercise in whatever way works best for you. Stretching and yoga, jogging, lifting weights, and even dancing are excellent ways to move your body and improve your heart health. The most crucial part is that you are moving and increasing your heart rate.

There is no shame in changing your workout routine if you find it's not enjoyable. Maybe you dread every run, so you try biking instead. Or perhaps you hate going on a treadmill but feel at peace running through nature.

It could even be that you normally go for thirty minutes, but today, you only feel up for fifteen. Do what makes you feel good, not what others say is *supposed* to make you feel good. Only you know your own body and mind.

It can also be helpful to have some sort of accountability. You can join a community sports team or ask a friend to be your running buddy. With someone else to make sure you show up, you are more likely to take that first difficult step of doing it. Once you've started, it's not as bad as you think.

Such habits can also be contiguous, and as a runner, I found that other team members started joining in, and it became their daily bread. At Innolead, the whole team participates in the Gaborone annual marathon. Besides being good for everyone's health, it also becomes a collective fun activity.

If you need extra motivation and can't find someone to work out with you, look into other ways to make it fun. Listen to your favorite music or podcast, try to beat your record time, play a game, and set small goals that are easy to attain, giving yourself a dopamine boost.

Another factor for the Blue Zones, the healthy areas of the world, is that people move naturally. They aren't necessarily going to the gym every day, nor are they regularly running marathons. Instead, they are physically active in their daily lives. They grow a garden or do housework without machines or other conveniences. Just like my grandfather and grandmother used to do all day with farm activities that required body movement!

That's not to say you can't be healthy by going to the gym, running on a treadmill, or lifting weights. That is a good way to keep active, and if you enjoy it, keep going. But if the gym or running isn't for you, consider how to add exercise to your preexisting lifestyle.

Some common ways are:

- Take the stairs instead of an elevator
- Get a standing or treadmill desk so you're not sitting all day, or use a mini bike that goes under your desk to pedal while you work.
- Plant a garden and do regular work in it.
- Go on walks during breaks & park farther from your work or the grocery store.
- If you are a social person, join clubs, go running, go cycling, do yoga, or play with your kids or pets.
- Do squats, lunges, or stretches in slow moments, like during a commercial or while brushing your teeth

Even fifteen minutes of daily exercise is 105 minutes a week. That's just under two hours!

Listen to your body to know if you're pushing yourself too hard or need to push a little harder. If a particular exercise doesn't feel good, don't do it, but don't be put off by feeling sore muscles the next day. As long as it isn't overly painful, your muscles are strengthening, and it's the only way you will be able to increase your fitness level.

Exercise, whatever way works best for you, and see the benefits. Experts agree that regular exercise provides the best immunity against diseases and contributes immensely to longevity.

Apply these strategies for EntreHappiness.

I have had many moments where I wondered if my business venture was all worth it, especially when I missed valuable time with my young kids. Sometimes, I was so focused on my start-ups that I was robbed of the joys of life.

I remember earlier in my journey when I came across an ad for a general manager at one of the diamond mines. It was extremely tempting as I thought, "Why should I go through all these troubles when I can earn a high salary at a corporation and stay away from such stress?" For days, I pondered going back, but the one thing that stopped me was the thought of losing control of my life—the freedom to dictate my life's purpose.

How could I return to the bureaucratic system I ran away from, taking away the ability to define my destiny?

Ultimately, I came to my senses and let this feeling pass. Good decision! I wouldn't be where I am today if I had given up.

In the last chapter, we learned about the JoyReP process. It can be used in any aspect of life, but it most definitely applies to entrepreneurs. We want sustaining and fulfilling success that will help keep us happy and satisfied for years to come. This is not found in the size of your bank account or your sales report!

You can get outside advice or encouragement by networking with other professionals in your field. My relationships with Martin Seligman, Clem Sunter, Salim Ismail, Louis Ferreira, and many others have been vital for my success both as an entrepreneur and as a human being.

There is every reason to make happiness a priority on your entrepreneurial journey. Take it from a man with decades of experience: it's never too late or too early to be happy.

Chapter Takeaways:

- Build life-giving moments of fun both in your work and personal life. Without ways to pour into yourself, you will be depleted by stressful circumstances that are out of your control.

- Focus on your physical and mental well-being. Challenges will inevitably come your way, but you should not sacrifice your health in order to take care of them.

- Happiness leads to success, not success to happiness. You cannot feel satisfied with life if you do not make happiness a priority.

CHAPTER SEVEN

UBUNTU: UNITY IN COMMUNITY

What counts in life is not the mere fact that we have lived.
It is the difference we have made in the lives of others that
will determine the significance of the life we lead.
—Nelson Mandela

When was the last time you helped a stranger? Or the last time you made a decision for the benefit of others, regardless of personal gain? When did you last say yes when a friend asked a favor, even if you had your own to-do list?

Ubuntu is an African philosophy that describes strong community values where "me" becomes "we." It has been translated as "I am because we are" and "A person is a person through other people." In Setswana, this is "*Motho ke motho ka batho.*" More than a philosophy, Ubuntu is a way of life.

I believe that Africa needs to:

1. Get back the Ubuntu values that make us who we are
2. Share those values with the rest of the world to counter the loneliness epidemic

Ubuntu is believed to have originated with the Bantu people and is particularly popular in Southern Africa, but it exists throughout the continent with slight variations. In Setswana, it is called "*botho.*" Many parts of Western Africa have a concept called "*biako ye,*" which means "unity is great."

Collaboration is not just encouraged; it is the very lifeblood that runs through the veins of Africa.

Nelson Mandela described Ubuntu as when a traveler stops at a village and is given food and water without even having to ask for it. The people of the community welcome him into their homes to make sure he has what he needs before he continues his travels. Such values still exist among many villagers across Africa; the warmth of the community can be felt.

The simplicity and power of Ubuntu cannot be understated. Ubuntu is about the interconnectedness of a community. We should have empathy and compassion for our fellow men because we are all human, and we cannot be our best selves without each other. We learn how to be a human from other humans—everything from walking and talking to dancing and singing!

As seen in the relationship part of the JoyReP concept, Ubuntu quite literally is one of the major keys to happiness! With this focus on community, individual needs are viewed as less important than the good of society. No single person should be thriving at the expense of others. Everyone has a voice. You are because of others!

The disrupted humanness in how we run business has caused havoc, resulting in the global mental health crisis. Entrepreneurs, especially those who are lonely during the start-up phases, are very vulnerable.

We would do better if Ubuntu were weaved through the ways of starting and running a business. It anchors you on the goodness of people and keeps you connected and humbled in a way that can keep away isolation, workaholism, and the associated negatives. It talks about good habits and character, human connections, being thankful, and being ready to show gratitude.

Ubuntu and Africa

In some ways, Ubuntu has slipped away from our African culture. Every day, African people die from poverty, hunger, and disease. Corruption and looting of countries' wealth by ruling elites are prevalent.

Why?

Because we have thrown away our age-long tradition, we let hatred, jealousy, war, and famine infiltrate the charitable culture we once had in Botswana. The old Kgotla democratic system of governance is premised on consultation (morero le therisanyo le morafe).

The old proverb says, "kgosi ke kgosi ka batho ba yone," translating to, "a king is king because of his people." This plainly underlies the democratic and consultative essentials ingrained in our systems.

At the time of writing, the people of Botswana had just voted out the party that had dominated Botswana politics for almost sixty years. Outside countries watched in awe and admiration as the transition was conducted peacefully when the new government took over. For us, it felt like just another day in Botswana!

Botswana is renowned as an icon of democracy in Africa and globally, and elections have been held peacefully every four years ever since our independence. Some say Botswana is not known globally because hardly any crisis or bad news comes from the country. This is all because the roots of Ubuntu still hold strong despite the harsh and corrosive winds of modernization threatening this value system.

Ubuntu lives simply in other ways because it cannot disappear from the human heart. Although we choose to move away from this beautiful inheritance due to blind Westernization of values, deep down inside us, there is Ubuntu. It is still alive, with the 2024 peaceful election being an example.

Goodness exists in all of us because we come from something good and are part of something bigger and better than ourselves. In other words, we are good because our maker is good. We just need to open our hearts and let Ubuntu reign supreme again.

In her Tedx Talk "Living Ubuntu; We Rise by Lifting Others," Gertrude Matshe describes Ubuntu as something she was never taught in her Zimbabwe home but something she saw and experienced.

In 2007, she noticed that kids at a local school were so exhausted they couldn't stay awake. The cause? They were only eating a couple of meals a week. So, she started a feeding program to give these students a meal. The problem came when parents began sending their younger children to access the food she provided.

Her solution?

She started a preschool, something uncommon in the area. Gertrude was already making a difference in the lives of many children through the feeding program, and she easily could have told the parents not to send the younger children so she could focus only on the older kids.

Instead, she sought a comprehensive solution to the problem because it benefited her community. She learned the value of just showing up and, in the process, inspiring young girls who saw a woman from their community taking the lead in a way women rarely could. A person because of others!

Another African who has gained traction for his Ubuntu-like values is Ghanaian actor-turned-farmer John Dumelo.[38] He uses social media platforms to advocate for agriculture, focusing on changing the youth's perceptions of farming and encouraging their involvement in the sector. 70% of employment in Africa is in agriculture, which supports the livelihood of millions of African families, especially women.

He sees that some younger generations pursued farming without realizing the challenges, making them more likely to change to a more predictable career. As a result, most of the farmer population in Ghana is older, which could lead to food insecurity in the future.

John Dumelo posts videos and helpful tips to encourage youth to see the joys of farming and to show them that any difficulties they face in the sector are manageable. As he advocates further for agriculture, he helps to reverse the food security crisis for future generations. He is making a difference through feeling for his people and taking action.

We've talked in previous chapters about the importance of fun, and Ubuntu is all about fun!

According to Lovemore Mbigi, an Ubuntu-focused author and philosopher, workers in a tobacco plantation in Zimbabwe celebrated harvest with song and dance.[39] This would increase their dopamine levels to prepare for the subsequent peak performance work. It boosted camaraderie and team connection. True fun and collectively are also ingrained in Ubuntu values, which contribute to happiness.

It's much easier to keep working when you've just danced to celebrate!

In rural Ethiopia, the coffee ceremony is a prime example of how Ubuntu is ingrained in African culture. Families and friends gather together in a living room or under a large tree to spend time together over freshly brewed coffee.

There are three rounds of coffee, the first being the strongest cup and the last being a light cup. Every detail, from the smell of the coffee to grinding the beans by hand, is a tradition designed to encourage connection.

Gossip, news, and wisdom are shared just as much as coffee. This ceremony can take several hours. The hands-on process allows time for extended conversations and promotes mindfulness and deep connections. Even at our farms in Botswana, I would observe our farm workers always coming together during their free days, spending hours upon hours under camel thorn trees enjoying tea and connecting.

Ubuntu is found in how we in Africa dance and sing together, tell stories around the fire, and visit each other for tea. If someone is sick or elderly, they will receive many visits throughout the day from friends and family who want to keep them company and help them get better. Mma Mmiga used to do that and take me along to visit unwell relatives and check on the elderly. Ubuntu is part of our African DNA.

Ubuntu and the World

In many ways, countries outside of Africa could use more Ubuntu in their cultures. The Western world as a whole focuses too much on the individual rather than the community.

Even Western media reflects this truth, especially in movies where the name of the main character is even the name of the film!

Disney films like *Moana,* superhero movies like *Spiderman,* and action-adventure films like *Indiana Jones* are named after the protagonist, who has some special talent or ability that makes them the only one who can save the day.

Even if they have help from side characters, the main character always comes up with a cunning plan to win the final battle. This teaches people they have to overcome their obstacles on their own, denying the invaluable support that the community can provide. The hero culture runs high in the Western world.

In fact, this is so ingrained in Western media that few high-ranking movies focus on a community of people helping each other.

Take the Disney classic *Finding Nemo.* Though Nemo and Marlin are the main characters, father and son reunited only with the help of Dory, the sea turtles, the sharks, the pelican, and the sea creatures in the dentist's tank. It is a

movie about a community coming together to help someone in need, even if that someone is entirely different from
them—as different as the predator shark and the prey fish.

By bringing our Ubuntu ideas to the Western world, we
could encourage them to work together. A classic Western
image of success is stepping on other people to reach the top
and pushing them down. Instead, we should get a boost from
other people and then turn around to pull them up.

We have already seen outstanding benefits when communities reflect Ubuntu values (even if they've never even heard
the word Ubuntu). In 2018, fifteen-year-old Greta Thunberg
made headlines with her passionate speeches advocating for
climate change prevention.

Across the world, young people joined together to protest government inaction. What began as one girl's passion
turned into a global movement that tied people together
worldwide. They fought for a better world for themselves
and future generations.

Other protests, such as Black Lives Matter, have brought
together communities who want social change in their countries. The French are known for their protests, commonly for
politics or working conditions. The 2024 agricultural protest
saw actions such as dumping manure and rotting produce in
front of government buildings. While the actions themselves
can be debated, it is clear the French know a thing or two
about demonstration!

Natural disasters also bring about a community effort.
Following hurricanes, tornados, wildfires, and other crises,
people raise money to aid those affected. Even people with
little to spare gather to support the communities who have
lost everything and can only get back on their feet with the
aid of others.

Another aspect is the mental health crisis that has taken
the world by storm. As discussed elsewhere in the book,

loneliness and rugged individualism are destroying people, leading to unnecessary early deaths and mental health problems.

We need to find a new global center to rediscover the value of "you are because of others." We are naturally social animals, and there is clear evidence that isolation and individualism are not serving us well. The principles of Ubuntu could offer a solution for returning to this basic human virtue.

The Western world has proved that communities can come together, but it's not enough. It should not be reserved for extreme cases but instead should be part of everyday life.

Ubuntu and Entrepreneurship

Ubuntu is not just a concept for the broader society. Its principles can be the difference between a thriving or struggling business. When employees don't feel supported by the community, they will not want to stay, which can lead to quiet quitting or actual quitting.

This is why I enjoy dancing with my employees at work, bringing the fun to an environment that could easily be dull. A strong community culture is linked to higher productivity and happier employees.

For example, Google is well-known not only as a thriving tech company but also as a great place to work. Their headquarters across the world have perks like free food, video game stations, mini golf, and nap pods. The company places a higher priority on employees' well-being and peace of mind, allowing anyone who needs it to take a break and come back refreshed.

Netflix is known for its time-off benefits, giving unlimited vacation time and up to 52 weeks of paid parental leave. This allows employees to spend time with family and, therefore, feel supported both at home and in the workplace.

Our daughter-in-law Erin in Ottawa was able to take twelve months of parental leave to care for their first daughter, Nakani, and even my son was able to take parental leave to attend to family needs at this sensitive time for the family.

These are examples of Ubuntu at play, and it is a pity that we in Africa don't even have such arrangements in our policy frameworks. Africa needs to Ubuntu her governance policies!

It's not just the big companies that can find success. *Business Insider* released a list of the twenty-five best-rated small to midsize companies for work culture, all of whom have less than 500 employees.[40]

One of the most common praises for those best-rated companies was that the team felt like a family that always supported each other in a real Ubuntu style. Maybe they can't have nap pods and video games on the same scale as Google, but they can still form strong, trusting relationships that lead to future success.

Not only are smaller companies equally capable of having a strong work culture, but big-name companies do not always have good working conditions.

Amazon is notorious for its poor work culture. Speed is the focus, with employees needing to complete tasks in a certain amount of time, or they could be in trouble. Another issue is micromanaging, which means that anytime an employee makes a mistake or doesn't complete a task within the designated time, they are investigated and potentially reprimanded.

There have even been reports of Amazon employees peeing in bottles instead of going to the bathroom so they can keep up with quotas.

The difference between a good work culture and a bad one is treating employees like they are human beings and not just another part of the assembly line. They have families that may be going through challenges, and they have basic human needs to be taken care of.

Employees should not be peeing in bottles or getting reprimanded for unexpectedly taking time off to go to a funeral. If company leadership followed Ubuntu, they would recognize how their own humanity relates to the humanity of those around them.

As Robert Anderson and William Adams say in *Mastering Leadership*, the best leader is a "radical human," a person who embraces unity with others through vulnerability and love. When I came across this comprehensive research, I concluded that leaders need Ubuntu training to make them not just human but to produce results!

Ubuntu in Action

One of the lowest moments in my entrepreneurial life was when about fifty of my cattle were stolen by a trusted farm foreman.

I recruited Mafense when he was twenty-two years old, and over the next fifteen years, he worked himself up to farm foreman. He consistently demonstrated dedication to farming, hunger to learn, and strong leadership skills. We supported his children's education and allowed him and his wife to attend farming courses at the local agriculture university.

Remember that cattle theft is one of the biggest crimes in most African countries because cattle are a highly-revered asset. His theft, which took place over the course of two years, was a major blow to me. He had betrayed my trust in him.

It especially tested my commitment to trusting my team members, even tempting me to doubt those at our sister companies, Innolead and DigitalGae. Every time he loaded up my cattle and sold them to other farmers, he took advantage of my trust.

The last sale took place in June 2023 when he loaded seventeen cattle from the farm. Someone tipped off the police, and I was called to witness the cattle in the village Kgotla, the public meeting, where they kept stray and stolen cattle.

As calmly as I could, despite my anger, I greeted Mafense and his wife, Kitso, when they were handcuffed in police custody. As required by law, the cattle were identified by witnesses, including the police and the village chief.

Afterward, I drove the three hours back to Gaborone on a lonely, quiet road. To lift my spirits, I decided to play my favorite music, and soon, I was singing and dancing in the car to songs by Public Enemy, Grandmaster Melle Mel, and some regional songs by TKZee and Trompies.

Even though I was facing one of my most difficult entrepreneurial challenges, I was able to find a temporary boost in happiness because of my love for music.

In the middle of this long drive and music blasting, I called Thobo (pseudonym), one of my music-loving friends. He was surprised I was in such high spirits despite my anger about the cattle. He was also not happy with me for traveling such a daunting trip alone in such a state!

Thobo immediately asked me to join him and another friend for drinks at the local clubhouse when I got back, and we spent that evening laughing and relishing in the joy of being together. I received firsthand social support when I needed it most. I managed to vent about the whole episode while they actively listened and assured me it was not all lost. And indeed, we had each other!

We can see Ubuntu (and the lack thereof) in two ways in this story. First, Mafense did not show Ubuntu values when he stole the cattle. He knew how serious this crime was, but he went so far that he stole from someone who was helping his family with education!

We can contrast this with the story in Chapter Two of the senior herdboy Tsimako, who was whipped for losing the cattle. His loss was an accident, but he humbly accepted the punishment. Ubuntu is about accepting responsibility for your actions, including your unintentional mistakes.

On the other hand, we can also see Ubuntu portrayed in my experience with Thobo. Knowing how upset I must have been, he caringly reprimanded me for taking the drive alone and invited me to spend time with friends. In this joyful time together, we found solace in the community despite the challenges we were facing.

Ubuntu and happiness are directly related. If we spend all of our time outside the community, we will be internally miserable. We can climb our way to the top by stepping on and over other people, but no matter how much external "success" we have, we will not be happy.

We need to recognize our place in the world amidst the people around us, not disconnected but interconnected.

In the town of Roseto, Pennsylvania in the 1900s, scientists and researchers discovered a key to longevity that looked like it was taken right from the Ubuntu book.[41] A group of Italian Americans had emigrated to the United States a few decades prior.

In the 1960s, a local physician noticed that all his patients from Roseto exhibited an almost shocking level of excellent health. Despite the fact that most of the men worked long hours and their families ate lots of pasta, smoked, and drank copious amounts of red wine, there was a surprising lack of heart attacks in this specific community.

The study showed that in Roseto, the rate of heart attacks in people over sixty-five was half the national average, and for those under fifty-five, there were no cases of heart attacks.

There was one indicator that explained everything: relationships. Their strong social connections displayed a high level of ethnic and social homogeneity, close family ties, and cohesive family relationships. When I read this, I became nostalgic for our old village culture where everyone was family. In our traditional culture, "the village raises all children," and all elders are parents.

So, the Roseto community lived a lifestyle and value systems that are similar to many villages still in Africa. Big families that live with and near each other are close-knit communities where trust, religion, loyalty, and solidarity are highly valued. The Roseto community also loved fun; regular boisterous parties and get-togethers with lots of wine were very common.

Ubuntu in Action!

But the Roseto community didn't stay this healthy. The pressures of modernization caught up with them, and their health now resembles that of the American national averages. Like us in Africa, they succumbed to the pressures of the nuclear family, no longer living in multigenerational homes but instead moving to isolated suburban neighborhoods.

The message is clear that we need to weigh social connections equally with other health and well-being practices. I encourage you to plan social gatherings in your schedule as much as you can. It may just give you a couple of years longer on Mother Earth.

So, the Roseto Effect is synonymous with the Ubuntu effect. Let us learn from these noble and simple case studies, integrate these into our lives, and bend the curve of mental health crises toward a happier and better life in society.

A similar phenomenon is found in the Blue Zones, areas in the world with the highest concentration of centenarians. In addition to factors like diet, one common thread is that they typically put their family first.

The longer people live, the more likely they are to have an emphasis on human connection in their lives. They feel a sense of belonging in their community, and older generations stay at or around home instead of being pushed out of sight in a nursing home. This idea can be seen in the Netflix documentary *Live to 100: Secrets of the Blue Zones.*

Ubuntu is the biggest key to happiness, not just in the entrepreneurial world but in daily life. We need to focus on our impact on the community and our unique power to give back to society. If everyone is looking out for themselves, only you will have your interests in mind, but if everyone is looking after everyone else, then millions of people would be thinking for your benefit.

Ubuntu empowers you to find satisfaction not in what you can do for yourself but in what you can do for others.

Chapter Takeaways:

- A thriving society is one in which the community looks after both friends and strangers, treating everyone as valuable people.
- Businesses should focus on the health of employees, creating a supportive and relationship-driven work environment.
- People are scientifically proven to live longer when they have strong community relationships, and they are better able to fight their battles if they do so with the help of others instead of on their own.

CHAPTER EIGHT

TEN BIGGEST CHALLENGES FOR ENTREPRENEURS

They tried to bury us. They didn't know we were seeds.
—Dinos Christianopoulos, Greek poet

The road to entrepreneurial success is littered with thousands of victims who went to an early grave, slipping into depression, substance abuse, and broken relationships. Operating in highly regulated markets like Africa and smaller populations like Botswana can be daunting.

These markets are unlike the mega markets that thrive on ideas and innovations, like Silicon Valley in California. Operating in large cities like San Francisco, New York, London, Tokyo, or Shanghai can make a big difference because of the sheer size of those economies. The smaller markets make it tougher and more stressful to achieve one's entrepreneurial dreams, a phenomenon I have witnessed personally.

Entrepreneurs are hungry to succeed. A seemingly wise and noble aspiration, but if not done properly, it can come with devastating consequences. The desire to do great things can lead to bad habits. Once we have our eyes on a vision, we don't stop, even at the cost of unsustainable hours and social isolation.

The entrepreneurial journey is not known for being easy. You will have moments full of triumphs that leave you excited for the future, but you will also encounter obstacles that leave you deflated. Any turn can test your creativity and resilience in unforeseen ways. From feeling alone to getting investors and support, we'll explore the common hurdles, as seen in the line of entrepreneurs.

You can prepare for these inevitable future hurdles by making yourself aware of them and planning accordingly. While you can't know for sure which of them you will face, you can look at your past to see what similar situations brought you down. Like me, you can use your past as fodder for strength and resilience.

Don't wait until you're at your lowest point to strategize for your future. By then, it may be too late to save you from addiction or life-threatening diseases. Let me share some of the dark sides of entrepreneurship, many of which I have lived through in my entrepreneurial life;

1. Self-Objectification

It all starts with what experts call self-objectification, a concept where you see yourself as an object of use for some future purpose instead of seeing yourself as a human being. It's also where you can use other people as a tool for achieving your own purpose.

It defies humanism, as described by Ubuntu, and reduces you or workers to things. Workers who see themselves used as tools and not recognized as agents in the working environment typically end up burnt out, depressed, and dissatisfied in their jobs.

According to Arthur Brooks, self-objection lowers self-worth and life satisfaction. The hyper-competitive, individualistic nature of our world makes this a problem for entrepreneurs striving to achieve big things. We Africans push even harder to catch up with our Western colleagues, who have better infrastructure and ecosystems to support them.

Entrepreneurs can become heartless drivers who harass workers to achieve an unnatural pace of work, all to achieve their narrow economic and material desires. At some point, they stop viewing their workers as people. I have heard many employees of ambitious entrepreneurs on how they get badly treated and how they are just pawns on the chessboard. Such mistreatment is not only unacceptable but detrimental to everyone's health and the growth of the business.

Self-objectification comes in when entrepreneurs do the same to themselves. They push past their limits so they can attain an unmanageable lifestyle that they think will make them happy.

Don't treat yourself as "the job" or an object! The JoyReP and EntreHappiness concepts provide a tool to prevent this. Be happy first, and success can come after.

Trevor Noah, host of the popular Daily Show in the US for seven years, is another example of a successful African. The South African confessed that his life became his job, leading to him feeling socially isolated from friends and loved ones.

The wrong type of success can lead us on the wrong path. It is this self-objectification that leads to many of the other problems we will talk about. So reflect on how you treat your staff and how you are treating yourself, and correct yourself when there is still time.

2. Success Addiction & Workaholism

Entrepreneurs are strivers who develop visions that make us picture our future selves as highly successful. Your ego can be pumped up by your teams, customers, competition, suppliers, the media, and even the government. This success definition can become an obsession.

According to Harvard Business Review, the average American CEO works 62.5 hours per week, versus 44 hours by the average worker.[42] I have done over 79 hours in a single week, grinding away in pursuit of happiness.

Such addiction to success leads to workaholism, which I confess I suffered with for many years of the start-up phase—with devastating effects on my family, friends, and health. This obsession led to tension with my wife, Nancy, when she requested I spend more time with her and the kids.

As much as I wanted to be with my family, I felt I was working hard so that they could have the best life, go to good schools, live in a bigger house, and get more holidays.

Don't we all say that?

Coming from a working-class family and more so a single-parent one, I was determined to make it! It was my mission to ensure my family would have a better life compared to the financial struggles my mother had.

Nancy loves to tease me, "I am still waiting for the future you promised us for years of toiling at Innolead!"

Entrepreneurs also tend to live in fear of failure. With all the glamor that goes with success, we feel we need to maintain or enhance this status by becoming the best in the industry or conquering other markets. When Innolead opened offices in other countries, I could see the pride in our people. This only put pressure on me not to fail!

I had always put my best into whatever I put my hands on, from my school grades to performing as an entrepreneur. My mother impressed upon me a perfectionist nature that did not help my workaholism. She would work through the night, committed to her students' success.

Simply put, success addiction is dangerous if not addressed. It's a very positional construct as it enhances our position in the social hierarchies, pushing away happiness. Unhealthy competition sets in, and even the money that comes does not buy the joy we seek.

We need to build our lives outside of work, prioritizing the things that truly make us satisfied. Revisit JoyReP for a more sustainable, happy self.

3. Social Comparison

Social comparison is by far the phenomenon that's going to tear apart our aspirations as Africans to close the gap with the developed world. It is a plague that has been eating away at our social fabric for centuries. We want to look like the leading executives on TV, driving the fanciest cars and choosing the most luxurious brands.

Meanwhile, millions of people live in poverty.

I'm no saint. Once in a while, I want the taste of good aged South African wine. As they say, life is too short to drink bad wine! Although I admittedly don't have the data to support this, I estimate that billions of dollars are lost in Africa to luxury items and other unproductive means instead of the innovation that will pave the way for our future.

A typical example is the convoy of expensive vehicles that our heads of state drive around while our people toil in poverty. How does that add up? It can only be the pressure of wanting to look the part and losing the purpose for which citizens vote for you: to improve their lives, not to look good in fancy black BMWs. This always baffles me, but I can only think it's the pressure to look like other heads of state in high-income countries.

It is not surprising that Africa lags behind with little funding for research and development or technology exports. Though I am not perfect, I decided earlier in my career to fight this. It is difficult to ignore all the beautiful and rich people paraded on social media every hour, but I remain humble and focused on my goals of improving social and economic development.

I seek to positively touch lives, like our farm workers, who for the first time have begun to experience decent levels of electricity, better housing, and even internet service in the middle of the African bush.

With our support, one of our farm worker's sons made it to university, a first for the family and one of the few in their village. This becomes self-reinforcing as it reminds me to keep away from the temptation of falling prey to social comparison pressures. It is very fulfilling to see the impact of your hard-earned money on uplifting other people's lives. Keeps me grounded and focused on my life purpose.

According to Sonja Lyubomirsky, the obsession with how others are doing is called the upward comparison, leading to distress, low self-esteem, and feelings of inferiority.[43]

A problem with us entrepreneurs is that we always look up to our role models. We often forget many of them started just like us. According to Sonja and her team, unhappy people are more inclined to compare themselves with people who are more successful. So let's quit the habit. This is a pattern that has made Africa dominate the top ten most unequal countries in the world. It's a very un-Ubuntu situation that needs reversal. The gap between the very rich and poor in countries like Botswana and South Africa is a scar that requires much introspection and reversal.

Social comparison can be insidious. Notice your reaction when you see a competitor driving a new car or moving into a new house. You need to be intentional and disciplined to counter the jealousy you feel.

The mark of someone who can resist the ugliness of social comparison is someone who is working to help others, not overly focused on themselves. I saw it with Mma Mmiga as she was always sensitive to helping those in need. As a result, she denied her desires and focused on the well-being and future of her kids, her students, and her wider family. Having a clear purpose in life can assist in pushing back this scourge.

She had a clear view of her future, which she was not willing to compromise by competing with other teachers, who were mostly married and well-off. They had cars, electrified houses, and TVs. My grandfather had the same attitude. Although he himself was well off, he would share with poor neighbors and employed large numbers of workers during harvest times.

We can't improve our societies if we are focusing on our personal gain and extrinsic goals of how the world sees us. And the more you do altruistic actions, the more you can resist the temptations.

Do your best to stay away from the social comparison pandemic. It will rob you of not only your happiness but also investments for your true future.

4. Substance Addiction

In this tough terrain, some entrepreneurs deal with stress by numbing themselves with substances. Unfortunately, even successful people fall for this problem as they think it could be a coping mechanism or a good escape. Entrepreneurial challenges provide the perfect storm to trigger the use of drugs. We can become stressed and isolated, leading to making unhealthy decisions like drinking a bit more or trying drugs.

According to the OECD, the likelihood of drinking rises with education levels and socioeconomic status.[44] And I have seen this at parties and get-togethers for high achievers, who sometimes overdrink as a way of dealing with daily stressors. High-pressure jobs like running a business can lead one to self-medicate with alcohol to hazardous levels with the hope of temporary relief.

I am particularly sensitive to alcoholism because of my alcoholic father. I have seen the harmful effects it has, not only on the individual but also on the family. I saw with my eyes how it led to abusive, irresponsible behaviors and a parent neglecting his family. Even worse, the long-term damage to one's health is irreversible.

When my father finally recovered from this life of alcohol and two strokes, he was regretful in a teary way. He was able to start his life all over again. According to the National Drug-Free Workplace Alliance, positive drug results in many American industries are higher than recent years.[45] The positivity rate for the non-safety-sensitive workforce is twenty-five percent higher than it was in 2012.

According to the National Center for Drug Abuse Statistics, half of Americans twelve or older have used illicit drugs at least once, with marijuana being all around the most used drug.[46] Even here in Botswana and the rest of Africa, drugs are landing in droves, and addiction problems are racking apart homes and families.

This is a serious problem that we can't let slide. Hundreds of thousands of people die from drug overdoses every year globally.

Addictions like this stop you from being present with your family, block you from making your businesses succeed, and take you away from true happiness. Entrepreneurs are very vulnerable to stress due to start-up challenges. And the temptation to numb themselves with drugs remains real. So stay strong and adopt the JoyReP formula for success and the EntreHappiness strategies. This will help you not only resist but also lead a life of energy and vitality.

If you are currently struggling with addiction, seek help.

5. Isolation

No good comes from being an entrepreneur who is alone. Because the company is in your hands, it can feel like the burden is only yours to carry. You may feel very lonely, but I have been there. That is far from the truth.

You can build a team that will help navigate the troubles you encounter, a team with unique skills that complement your own. Outside your work, you should also have a support system of your friends and family. These are people not directly involved in your business but who can help you stay motivated in the face of any difficulties.

I hope by now you understand how important this idea is to me. The theme of relationships is woven throughout my life now. I've already shared the struggles I faced in my thirties as a lonely entrepreneur who was not making time for relationships. In reality, I see my troubles with isolation much earlier.

When I was studying engineering in England, I was often shut up in my room, studying or doing homework for hours on end. My housemates, Prartha and Laura, would barge in and rescue me, taking me to the pub for some time off.

Studying overseas can be very lonely as you travel thousands of miles away from close family and friends. My friends were my support, making my four-year stay there very memorable. *The New York Times* once reported that women who had at least three friends had higher levels of life satisfaction.[47] True friends are essential for happiness and combating isolation and loneliness.

Now, I have several entrepreneurs that I mentor. Ben, who was running a construction and beauty business in the start-up phases, would call me randomly and say, "Mr. K, I just want to talk to someone, and you are the person that brings hope and assurance to me. I am running low with my start-up challenges." I would then just listen up, give words of encouragement, and relate to my story of start-ups. He would be so grateful afterward.

I am honored to provide the support for other entrepreneurs that I desperately needed at the start of my journey.

These people who can give an encouraging word or be a listening ear truly make a huge difference.

In his TEDx Talk "The dark side of entrepreneurship," Keaton Smith shares his story of depression as a result of the pressures of growing a business. The lowest moments in his career brought him to the brink of suicide as he wondered if his family would be better off without him.

Keaton was trying to overcome these obstacles on his own so as not to burden those around him. He was working two jobs, barely seeing his family. He describes one time when he was considering suicide and says he only made it through the night thanks to his wife's care.

In an effort to have this type of support at all times, he asked his close group of friends for voice messages of encouragement that he could go back to if he was feeling discouraged again.

Now armed with over twenty minutes of encouragement, he found that by leaning on the support of those around him, he was better able to handle the pressures of starting a business. That does not mean the problems went away entirely, but he was more prepared to face them when it got hard. It was his true friends and supportive wife who saved Keaton's day.

The worrying trend is that men are losing touch with how to make friends, and most are crying out for skills to make friends. No wonder the introduction of happiness courses at Havard MBA students was a hit and oversubscribed! People desire to learn these basic human skills that we've lost to our grandparents.

According to social scientist Scott Galloway, one in seven men in the USA does not have a single friend.[48] Staggering statistics on isolation and struggles to make friends.

So build your social support as much as you build your business, you will need friends and family from time to time to keep you resilient and happy.

6. Rejection

Although you may not want to hear it, you are going to face rejection as an entrepreneur. Likely, you have at some point in your life. Whether it be from a job, a relationship, or a school, we dread hearing that painful "No."

We often take this rejection to heart, but usually, it's not meant as a personal affront. The same is true of entrepreneurial rejection.

Maybe you ask a company for support, and they don't have the financial means to invest in you. Or maybe you don't get as positive of a reaction to the launch of your product or service as you wanted. It could be that customers don't need your product or simply don't realize how they really *do* need it, but either way, it's not a direct attack.

One reason we entrepreneurs take rejection so hard is that we pour so much of ourselves into our companies that they become an extension of ourselves. This is the danger of not having a degree of separation between you and your work.

But know that even though you face rejection, that does not mean you will never get that long-awaited "Yes!"

Though she is not an entrepreneur in the typical sense, J.K. Rowling's rejection story is applicable to anyone feeling like they've failed before they even started.[49] She was living as a single mother, working a variety of jobs during the time she wrote what would become the number one best-selling series of all time, *Harry Potter*.

After twelve publishers rejected the first book, J.K. Rowling finally got a publisher, and the rest is history. Not only were her books successful, but she was also able to negotiate in her favor for the rights of the movie, allowing her to have more control than most authors who sign a movie deal.

Even though she is a well-known author now, it took one disheartening year of trying to get a publisher before she was able to see the success of years of writing. J.K. Rowling knows what it means to face rejection, but because she kept believing in her book, she was able to prove that her idea was literally worth billions.

So don't let rejection lead you to quit prematurely. Keep going while applying JoyReP and EntreHappiness so that you rebound with a bang.

7. Cash Flow Issues

Cash flow issues can be a huge challenge for entrepreneurs because they're not always predictable. Your responsibility is to oversee investments and expenses. But sometimes, you can't control who is investing in you or what financial problems you may unexpectedly run into.

When you start out in a business, your focus will be on making enough money to launch, including getting investments. This in itself is a hassle but very important. Not every investor will like your idea enough to fund you, and they'll often have critiques meant to make your idea better. You'll have to sort out what advice is helpful for you and what advice goes against your vision.

After that, you'll need to build up your clientele. Depending on your type of business, a dilemma you may face is whether you take every customer or only the people who align with your company values. It is your choice if you want to work with an incompatible buyer until you can afford to say no or whether you stick to your values from the start.

One big way to attract the right patrons is by increasing advertisement in your target market and audience. Between social media, email, websites, and physical ads, you have a lot of options. Find what works for you and invest in it.

Even when your business succeeds, you can still face other cash flow problems. As they say, growth burns cash!

A change in the industry can cause customers to no longer desire your service, and a risky investment gone wrong can drain your funds. As an entrepreneur, you absorb the effects of these challenges. While you can lean on your partners and employees for help, you don't have the ability to just walk away and let someone else fix it.

Cash flows have been one of the biggest challenges in my career, like during the start-phase, the financial crisis in 2008, and, ironically, during growth periods as well. It seems to be a perpetual problem for entrepreneurs, and it makes you appreciate that cash is truly king.

There was a time when we built cash at Innolead, leading to the purchase of a tech company, DigitalGae, from an owner who was retiring. I made a mistake by investing all our saved cash in this venture, which later underperformed. Now, over six years later, we are still struggling to recover from overinvesting in one company acquisition. We learned to always keep some cash locked away either in equities, off-shore, or fixed deposit accounts.

During another period, we were again growing very well and investing heavily in growth opportunities. We invested in launches and new offices in Lusaka, Zambia, and we opened offices in Luanda, Angola, one of the most expensive places on earth!

We explored project management opportunities in the mines of the Democratic Republic of Congo, burning hundreds of thousands of dollars. It was our first time exploring these markets, so we were a bit naive as shortly after we signed these initiatives, we got into contractual issues, unmet promises, and currency devaluations, things that were alien to us in Botswana.

Such investments need to be balanced with good cash reserves to sustain the running of core business operations. Again, there was a big lesson on how innocent growth intentions can burn cash and time!

You don't get this kind of knowledge or experience in MBA classes!

When trying to get funding to launch Airbnb, co-founder Brian Chesky sent requests to seven Silicon Valley investors, all of whom would not invest. They didn't see the potential in an idea that had strangers coming to stay in people's homes, an idea seemingly unfitting for the Western world.

The turning point? The Airbnb team designed cereal boxes centered around then-presidential candidates Barack Obama and John McCain and served them as a breakfast option for customers.

Tech startup Y Combinator invested in Airbnb specifically because of these cereal boxes.[50] They went from having no investors to eventually becoming a Fortune 500 company all because they thought of an out-of-the-box way to attract an investor.

So without cash, even the most fantastic idea can stay on the shelf. Without cash reserves, it may be difficult to retain talent and invest in systems and infrastructure required to remain competitive.

If you are already operating, keep some cash locked away. If you own a start-up and you believe in your idea, the world is full of venture capitalists and angel investors looking for good ideas, so never tire of hunting!

If Chesky and the Google founders had so many rejections, that should motivate you to keep hunting.

8. Mental Health

Because of the relationships I neglected in my thirties, I faced many mental health issues. I was overworked and burnt out, not spending enough time with loved ones. I know how easy it can be for entrepreneurs to put so much of themselves in their company that they have nothing left for themselves.

In the end, if you are reaching this level of stress, you are only making it worse for your company. Anxiety and depression are two genuine issues that we don't talk about enough in the entrepreneurial community. We often think if we focus on our business now, we can care for ourselves in the future. But taking care of your mental well-being is not a luxury; it's a necessity.

I mentor and support a young lady in her thirties with her technology start-up business. She would beam while telling me about the future of her business, confident in her ability to get investors as a woman in a market that competes with cheaper Chinese technologies.

Then, after working for months with a client who had complete confidence in her product, the client went with another company that hadn't even been on their tender list at the start of the process! She was devastated.

When we met later to discuss this, my friend told me that she had been driving to work the previous week when she had felt sick and unwell. She called her mom, who told her to park the car by the side of the road to rest.

Instead, she drove to the parking lot of her office, where her dizziness got worse. She called her office staff to pick her up and rushed her to the nearest hospital, where she was diagnosed with exhaustion and stress after being admitted overnight.

The doctors told her that all her vital signs were in order and that the only explanation was that she was stressed from her work, to which she agreed. She was a young lady, and I told her about my experiences and how she needed to find strategies for coping and protecting herself from extreme levels of stress, as it could lead to worse situations.

It was such incidents and many other stories from entrepreneurs that inspired me to develop JoyReP and EntreHappiness strategies. Some could seem simplistic but have a huge impact on your well-being.

This is the story of many entrepreneurs out there.

Arianna Huffington founded *The Huffington Post*. As the editor-in-chief, she experienced extreme burnout and fatigue because she overworked herself to her breaking point, a similar story to my young lady friend.

She finally realized just how much of a problem this was when the exhaustion caused her to collapse on her desk, hitting her head and breaking her cheekbone. Now, Arianna Huffington is an outspoken advocate for mental health, drawing on her own experiences as proof.

After her collapse, she examined her own life and the stressors she faced on a daily basis, leading to her publishing a book called *Thrive,* and to found Thrive Global, a platform to promote well-being. The situation she went through was a low moment in her life, but she has turned it around as a growth point to teach others the value of taking care of themselves.

Your business needs the healthiest, most productive version of you. Constantly pushing yourself beyond your limits will only lead to your decline, both physically and mentally. Your family and your company need you to be present and healthy.

Don't hurt yourself for the sake of your business. Your health comes first. It's the only thing you have.

9. A Wandering Mind

The problem with being a consultant is that I'm always a contrarian, challenging everything in my analytical mode. As a result, I am not always present in conversation or even while just trying to relax.

My wife, Nancy, has caught me contemplating an idea, not paying attention to her when she is talking to me. It has been a big weakness for me as it has robbed me of time with family, even when we are on holiday.

I also have very inquisitive kids, who have also inherited my curiosity. They read philosophers like Nietzsche and Carl Jung. The breakfast table is full of noisy debates on how to live or not live.

Our last born, Mbako, is more inclined to psychology, while our middle boy, Motheo, is the start-up guy who discusses business ideas. Our daughter, Fifi, is also reading books on stoicism and many self-help books that we debate about. Nancy, as a climate change and sustainability expert, leads hot debates about anything from Trump's and Al Gore's positions on climate change to what Africa should be doing on biodiversity.

It's an exciting family dynamic where we debate openly, and our kids feel free to express their thoughts. But it also disturbs good sleep if I get excited about an idea and can't calm down my brain. Nancy is brilliant at being able to switch off, relax, and be in the moment.

When we go on holiday, I have to plan activities every day so I can keep busy, much to her disgust. We once had a holiday in the Okavango Delta. I booked daily drives to check buffaloes and lion kills while Nancy slept in and relaxed. It was during that holiday that she talked to me about being able to sit down and do nothing. "Learn how to do nothing and relax," she would say. A tough call for a wandering mind.

This contradicts my natural tendency, but I have gotten better over the years. I am now able to sit like my grandfather Motuba at the farm under a tree, doing nothing for hours. It takes introspection, but it is important to simply exist in the moment without thinking about your business or your next big idea. It's calming and reduces brain fog.

10. Need for Control

As I already mentioned, you pour pieces of yourself into your business, so it makes sense that you might have a hard time giving up control. However, the entrepreneur who is obsessed with controlling every detail is denying that business the opportunity to grow.

If you are the only one who handles the important behind-the-scenes work, you are ensuring that your company will not survive if you're unexpectedly gone.

Your team is there to help you. Delegating tasks is one of the best ways to make sure your company is not dependent on you, and it can also ensure everyone is engaged in their work. It can be tempting for an entrepreneur to try to do everything in the business because you are the founder and owner. Although that can be done during the early start-up phases, it does not work once one of the employees grows and needs to delegate.

As we talked about in Chapter Four, you have the power to take tasks that are boring to you and give those to someone else. What is not your Unique Ability, you can delegate to a team member for which it is their Unique Ability. By knowing the strengths of your employees, you can make sure everyone is doing a job that suits them, and you can take some of the weight off your shoulders.

It can be extremely difficult to let go. It can be a painful process because you designed everything, and you feel you know how everything works. But sticking to controlling everything can only do damage, not only to the business but to your health and well-being.

When Innolead grew to over twenty employees, I had to start letting go of advertising accounts and operations. I had to recruit an operations manager and finance manager as I focused on the CEO role, business development, and new opportunities. When it works, it's a wonderful feeling, and you get to have more free time for rejuvenation, a critical aspect of happiness.

By the time we reached over fifty employees, we had a full management team holding its own executive team meetings without me as the Executive Chairman. Now, I have time to explore new 10x growth concepts, like exponential organizations, develop new products for growth, and start a podcast to share our amassed wisdom from the past twenty-five years of existence.

Oprah Winfrey may be a self-made billionaire, but that doesn't mean she works on her own. She needs a team of people to produce the Oprah Winfrey Network, which seeks to empower viewers to live their best lives. She continues to support weight loss programs and advocates for education, children, and women.

Oprah is quoted as saying, "Are we limiting our success by not mastering the art of delegation?" She knows that no good can come from an entrepreneur who wants total control over every aspect of their business. By working together, a team of people can ensure that a dream becomes reality.

So when the time is right, start letting go, hunt for who can cover other parts of the business, and let growth flow. The business is still yours!

You can overcome these challenges.

We often view the most successful entrepreneurs and companies—the extraordinary few who made it without difficulty—as superstars. However, all these people have been entrepreneurs just starting out, unsure of what would happen next.

Next time you feel discouraged, read through the stories of some of the most famous entrepreneurs. The names above are only the start of some celebrities who struggled to start a business. Bill Gates, Steve Jobs, Walt Disney, and even Thomas Edison failed at first.

The best time to prepare for these challenges is right NOW. Start building your support system, take care of your mental health, and come to terms with the truth that your journey will not always be easy. As you look at the difficulties ahead, keep an optimistic mindset so that when those hardships come your way, you already have a defense against them.

It may take some time for you to see success, so don't let the stress make you give up on your dreams too soon. Your idea is worth pursuing.

Use this therapist approach to quickly check if you are a Workaholic:

1. Do you usually spend your discretionary time on work activities?
2. Do you usually think of work when not working?
3. Do you work well beyond what is required of you?

In addition to the above, it becomes truly workaholism when you fail to reserve energy for your loved ones after work. They get the leftovers every day! Assess yourself, and be honest. Progress starts with the truth.

Chapter Takeaways:

- You will face challenges, but preparing now can make them easier when they come.
- Surround yourself with people who give you encouragement. You don't have to go through this alone.
- You will likely face rejection, but that doesn't mean you will never succeed. Keep pushing through, refining your idea, and waiting for that first "Yes!"
- Your mental health is more important than your business. Take care of yourself first, then use your renewed energies to support your growing company.
- Have confidence in your ability to make your dreams come true.

PART THREE
THE GIFT OF NOW

CHAPTER NINE

HARNESSING TODAY'S INNOVATION FOR A BRIGHTER TOMORROW

Tomorrow belongs to people who prepare for it today.
—African Proverb

I truly believe that it's a gift to be alive right now.

With each new invention, our world is getting better. We have the privilege of living in the midst of thrilling technological breakthroughs like artificial intelligence and stem cell research.

Compared to fifty years ago, when I was a young kid, we have a greater understanding of how the world works. We are more aware of climate change and its effects, we place a higher importance on mental health, and we realize our actions have led to the extinction of some species.

Never would young me have imagined that in my lifetime, I'd be able to have a real-time video conversation with people from around the world or that I could watch videos, send messages, and take pictures with the portable screen in my pocket.

Even with all the improvements, the world is not without problems. That's where entrepreneurs come in. By harnessing our natural creativity, we tackle the faults of this world head-on.

Armed with optimism and determination, we pave the way for a brighter future. In order to do so, we need to find the convergence of everything we talked about in this book so far. In the midst of endurance and happiness, we will find the gift of NOW.

Lifespan to Happierspan

In recent years, the term "healthspan" has seen an increase. While a person's lifespan refers to how long they live, health span refers to how long they are in good health.

I take this a step further and use the term "Happierspan," which refers to how long a person is happy. Poor health makes happiness harder, but a person can still be happy in the face of unfortunate health circumstances, such as I have had to do with my cancer diagnosis. JoyReP and EntreHappiness strategies can lead you to Happierspan–longevity with fun and vitality.

A powerful example of this is Chris Nikic, who became the first person with Down syndrome to complete an Ironman triathlon, a race that combines swimming, biking, and running.[51]

He had a goal to improve by 1% every day of his training. He wanted to change the stereotype that people with his condition couldn't do anything. Even after challenges such as open heart surgery as a child and delayed development, he pursued athletics and did not accept the limits others put on him.

Health and nutrition are incredibly important. If we are not eating healthy, working out, getting enough sleep, and going to the doctor, we are not taking care of ourselves. Similarly, excessive worry and isolation can lead to poor mental health and have even been known to worsen many illnesses.

Certain health issues are more of a risk with age, such as blood pressure, diabetes, and loss of tissue mass. We need to be on the lookout for these so we can catch them early. While we are still young, we can focus on our diet, exercise, and sleep, which can negatively impact us if we are not taking care of them.

Despite some bad habits and my battle with cancer, I am overall in good health, as I talked about in Chapter Four. I still have lots of energy, which allows me to dance, be active at work, and keep up with a vibrant life. I take the supplements I need to keep me in top condition. At age fifty-five, the game is only beginning.

We often think that once we reach a certain age, we are no longer able to break records, achieve dreams, or redefine possibilities. However, for a select few, age does not impact the ability to test their limits. In fact, age is often associated with wisdom, and who better to change the world than the wise?

J.R.R. Tolkien was between sixty-two and seventy-three when he published *The Lord of the Rings* trilogy, which is the second greatest book series of all time, according to *Forbes*.[52] [53] Colonel Sanders was sixty-five when he founded KFC after failing in several careers.[54]

According to the Guinness Book of World Records, the oldest college graduate is Shigemi Hirata at ninety-six years old.[55] Although he was not recognized by Guinness for failing to provide a birth certificate, Fauja Singh is recognized as the oldest person to have run a marathon at one hundred.

The United States even holds a National Senior Games where adults over the age of fifty can compete in Olympic-style games.[56]

Age does not limit what you can do. As long as you're still alive, you have a purpose! These inspiring seniors would not have changed the world if they thought they were done with their lives at age sixty. That is why the word "retirement" is out of my vocabulary. I am in the game all the way.

Wellness is especially important for entrepreneurs. We commit ourselves to life-changing goals, and if we pass early due to poor health, we are denying the world the benefit of our ideas. By living long and happy lives, we can enjoy the outcome of our hard work.

I believe that retiring should not be our goal. If someone is not physically able to continue in their current work, they can reassess, revise their purpose in life, and take on a new calling. Make your contribution by leveraging your unique skills all the way to the last breath.

Even if an older person chooses to retire from their previous career, they should not just sit around and do nothing. Any work that benefits the world around them is worthwhile, including dedicated volunteer work. But if they can, they should stay involved in their career field and keep making positive contributions to their industry.

It is important to keep your cognitive abilities going lest they become lazy. Risking ailments like dementia unfortunately led to the passing of my dear mother. Recall the Boston men longitudinal study in Chapter Five. The men who stayed at work into their eighties lived much longer lives.

Our Abundant Future

The world is constantly evolving.

We are living in the most technologically advanced period ever. With better healthcare, we are increasing life expectancy, and we can even target medical treatment to a person's specific DNA.

Stem cells have uses in regenerative medicine, blood disorders, and tissue repair. AI can scan medical data, while

Telehealth allows a patient to talk to a doctor without having to go into an office, which gives quicker access. Soon, medications will be available to everyone, everywhere.

Technology futurist Ray Kurzweil predicts that within ten years, we will have reached "longevity escape velocity," where we will start reversing the aging process so that a human can have a better healthspan and lifespan. He especially believes that artificial intelligence will surpass human intelligence and will, therefore, make incredible breakthroughs that we cannot imagine.

In *Abundance: The Future is Better Than You Think*, Peter Diamandis also discusses the idea that emerging scientific progress will allow for the end of problems like poverty and hunger. The more we expand our capabilities as a society, the more we can use our developments to help others.

It is a really exciting time to be alive, especially for entrepreneurs!

All we need to do is leverage future innovation to our benefit. This is seen in the concept of 10x technologies, which refers to new emerging technologies such as AI, drones, quantum computing, nanotechnology, and synthetic biology. These technologies grow in capabilities and reduce their costs exponentially. Our most ambitious goals can finally be realized right now due to the abundance of these technologies.

This has encouraged optimists like the Strategic Coach co-founder, Dan Sullivan, who plans to live to be 156 years old! He just celebrated his eightieth birthday this year and has rolling twenty-five-year plans, which include publishing a book every quarter. He lives a purpose-driven life that encapsulates longevity and well-being strategies.

The younger generations show a growing excitement for future science, including artificial intelligence. My son, for example, has been recruited by a top university in the United

Kingdom to work on his PhD researching AI in education because of the GreyEd education product he has invented.

However, it is not just the young adults that can take advantage of this. Older adults often think it is too late for them to learn new programs, but you are never too old to adopt modern innovation.

Technology is not the only great thing about this time period. In *Better Angels of Our Nature,* Steven Pinker asserts that despite some contrary beliefs, we are living in one of the least violent time periods in history. Thanks to empathy, self-control, and reason, we have taught ourselves to reduce our innate violent tendencies.

One reason people often believe the world is more violent than it is, according to Pinker, is the media. We have access to news from across the world, something that was unimaginable before phones.

Because of this, we see story after story of a violent event in another country and assume that there is a rise in such events. On the contrary, Pinker suggests that we are simply more aware of the violence that was always there. Less violence and conflict mean more time for creativity and impacting lives.

Another issue is our tendency to pay attention to bad news sooner than good, a phenomenon known as negativity bias. We may see a heartwarming story on the news, but the story that will stick in our minds is the latest shooting or political unrest. Because we often gravitate toward these negative headlines, news sources release more of this type of coverage so they can increase viewer count.

Sadly, most of the news regarding Africa is bad news about famine or conflict zones. This is bound to have a negative psychological impact on our people and even instill self-doubt. That is why I have stopped watching these "crisis news" channels, and I now go to bed in a much better mood than in the past when I used to watch CNN and BBC. I instead watch the UK's *Strictly Come Dancing*, comedies and history or wildlife documentaries.

Despite the many positive effects of living in an advanced world, we should be cautious even as we are hopeful. In his book *Suicide*, 19th-century French sociologist Émile Durkheim described what he found to be four types of suicide and their causes, including modernization.

Durkheim explained that a change in the economic state can disrupt social norms, causing people to question where they fit in society. This means that the more quickly a society modernizes, the more people will struggle to adapt.

Similarly, Swiss philosopher Jean-Jacques Rousseau observed in the 18th century that as people moved from rural, farming areas to urban, city life, they were less happy. They lost close communities and instead were thrown into a fast-paced world filled with corruption and greed.

There is something insidious about development that steals our souls.

If we're not careful, modernization can take our joys here in Africa. That's why it's important to first focus on happiness using EntreHappiness and JoyReP. These strategies can mitigate what both Rousseau and Durkheim observed in the past centuries.

Once you are secure in your happiness, you can make the most of modern innovation, which truly does offer amazing benefits. As with most things, the problem is not the technology itself but rather how we adapt to and handle it.

In Chapter One, I talked about my work with Clem Sunter, who was involved in futuristic e-planning. His goal is to advise governments and businesses on using past patterns to prepare for future challenges and opportunities. By putting preventive measures in place now, we can stop our companies from taking a hit later.

For example, we have encouraged the mines in Botswana to diversify from diamonds. Although this resource is responsible for much of our country's progress now, we know that it is finite. The planning for the post-diamond Botswana economy needs to start now, especially with the LGDs (or lab-grown diamonds) starting to eat into the natural diamonds market share. As experts say, no country has ever industrialized using a mineral economy!

The same can be applied to your business and even your life as a whole. Industry standards can tell a lot about what problems you may face in the future, and your most repeated mistakes point to what errors you will make tomorrow.

If you look at previous hurdles as singular instances, you hurt your ability to fight them more easily in the future. You can develop a few plans to exploit the future for your benefit. Futureproof starting now, at individual, organizational, and country levels.

Innovation in Africa—It's Our Time

With the help of my friend Salim Ismail, I am working to bring new technology to Africa so we can close the gap between this continent and the Western world. This cannot be done by someone in an office far away in the Western world; instead, we Africans need to be on the ground.

When I worked at Geoflux as a shareholder and director, I struggled to fit in and ended up quitting to go on my own.

I then started Innolead, where I was finally able to be my own boss by offering consulting services. It was freeing to be on my own. I was able to form a company that centered around my unique abilities and help organizations grow and compete.

That was in the early 2000s. In 2008, I started Manenzo Farming, keeping in line with my passion for nature, as we already discussed, and as part of my heritage from my grandfather Ramotuba. In 2017, we decided to invest in technology through DigitalGae Technologies, which was the acquisition of a pre-existing company.

That leads us to where we are now. We continue to seek growth both in the company and for each employee personally. In fact, that is where Innolead got its name. I always try to think creatively and build excitement around new ideas. We challenge ourselves to think innovatively and lead in the markets we operate in. Specifically, we lead with innovation. Inno and lead.

Even our logo focuses on the fun I try to incorporate. I designed it to look like someone standing on his head, recalling my breakdancing days. It literally shows fun! My business was to be run professionally but characterized by fun.

We need more innovation, leadership, and fun in Africa. We need to reverse the negative happiness rankings and create a happier continent to accelerate the 10x growth of the continent.

Approximately 600 million people in Africa don't have access to electricity. This is double the population of the United States. There is also an unsettling lack of quality education and extreme poverty rates in many countries. But it doesn't have to be this way. The gap can be closed NOW in the next ten to fifteen years. We don't have to wait fifty years to help our African people.

Africa is estimated to have a population of two billion by 2050, and this should provide ample opportunities for young people and entrepreneurs alike. It should not be a burden to have such a large population but an opportunity that can be exploited to lift Africans to join high-income economies of the world.

Even with the challenges, people here are making a difference.

1. **Temie Giwa-Tubosun** is the founder of the Nigerian company LifeBank. They use drones, bikes, and boats

to deliver blood, oxygen, and medical consumables across the country. Their work has allowed medical facilities in previously inaccessible areas to get life-saving supplies.[57]

2. **Ashish Thakkar** started his entrepreneurial journey at the age of fifteen. He started a small IT business that has since expanded with a presence in twenty-five African countries and spanning a variety of sectors. Among other ventures, one of his passions is encouraging other entrepreneurs, as he does with his app Mara Mentors, which pairs beginner entrepreneurs (often youth) with successful ones.[58]

3. **Bethlehem Tilahun Alemu** is the founder of the Ethiopian business soleRebels. Using locally sourced materials such as recycled tires, the company makes shoes through indigenous techniques. What started as a company employing a few people has expanded to hundreds of employees from her community. Her purpose was to create jobs and to build an Ethiopian brand when so many products she saw came from other countries.[59]

4. **Thione Niang** migrated to the United States in his early twenties after growing up in a Senegalese family of twenty-eight children. He worked behind the scenes in the political field, eventually working directly with President Barack Obama. After a few years, he moved back to Senegal and founded Jeufzone, an agricultural business that seeks to provide food for African countries and encourages young people to start agribusinesses. He also started a lighting company with Akon, a music star, and Samba Bathily, another entrepreneur. They have installed solar street lights and home systems in eighteen African countries.[60]

5. **Ushahidi** is a Kenyan crowdsourcing platform that has amplified its capability for change across the world. After the 2010 earthquake in Haiti, Ushahidi created interactive maps for people to report emergencies such as injuries or trapped people. The platform has also been used in the 2011 Japan earthquake and tsunami and for many countries during the COVID-19 pandemic.[61]

Africa is catching up slowly with the help of a community of people. Together, we can pull these people out of their difficulties and give them the tools they need to help the world.

Think about how many entrepreneurs there currently are in the United States. Africa's population is nearly four times that of the US, which means four times as many entrepreneurs are possible. Imagine how many of them are struggling right now because they don't have the resources they need to make a difference!

We don't have the same trajectory as Western countries. In fact, we have much to learn from them so we can refine our development model for education, work, and other systems. We need start-up ecosystems that can facilitate access to funding, technology, and talent.

But our Ubuntu-driven happiness can be stimulated by the innovative values of the West. By combining our family-oriented values with modern technologies, we can change the fate of the entire continent. It's time to take our happiness into our own hands. Let's define our own destiny, and others will start learning from us.

Entrepreneurs quite literally have the power to change the world. And now, we have to own our future.

Will you join me and the other entrepreneurs I mentioned above?

Chapter Takeaways:

- We need to be in the best of health so we can live long lives and make a difference in our community and the world.
- We are living in the most advanced and least violent society ever. We need to take advantage of the opportunities around us, which are found in modern technologies.
- Africa is behind in many ways, but we can blaze ahead if we use recent advancements to our benefit. As long as we keep in mind our community-driven values, modernization is the best way to get our people out of poverty.

CONCLUSION

CREATE & OWN YOUR FUTURE NOW

Philosophy is about turning words into works.
—Seneca

An entrepreneur's life isn't easy, but it also isn't impossible. We face challenges and heartaches. There are moments when we aren't sure if we will ever get our business off the ground. Statistics are also not on our side as the large majority fail. We feel isolated and rejected, our mental health suffers, and we just want our big idea to be released into the world.

But we also get to experience pure triumph and joy. There is nothing like the feeling of getting your first investor or customer. You rejoice at each year's increase in profit and every new perfect-fit employee.

Even better when you make an impact in your society by growing a company, creating employment, and paying taxes to develop education, health, and other social amenities. That's what we have done with our group of companies over the past twenty-five years. Living the purpose and achieving fulfilling success.

That doesn't make the restless nights easier, but it does make them worth it.

What is most important for anyone, not just entrepreneurs, is pursuing happiness. Without it, trivial things like success or important things like health are not possible. We can make money and watch our company become the biggest in the world, but if we are not happy, none of it matters.

Together, we can help everyone around the world who is struggling with a start-up. You may be ready to give up. Your family may be suffering alongside you. You may think it's hopeless. But there *is* hope.

We all reach low moments with tragic losses. We know how Anthony Bourdain and Kate Spade ended up taking their lives. I watched Anthony Bourdain on Netflix and was a big admirer of his work. Traveling the world, meeting people, eating exotic foods, he seemed so happy! But I got to understand his workaholic nature, which ended in tragedy.

Even one of Botswana's renowned transport and logistics magnates committed suicide, to the shock of the whole country. He was regarded as one of the most successful entrepreneurs in Botswana for decades. We are all vulnerable to mental health challenges.

We can imagine the millions across the world suffering from mental challenges due to the obstacles we face. You can stop this with EntreHappiness and JoyReP. Rediscover your fun, pursue relationships, broaden your world, and focus on your health.

These habits can build not only resilience and grit but also ignite the energies and creativity required for your teams and enterprise. But you need to be ready to change. As Albert Einstein said, "The measure of intelligence is the ability to change." Turn these words into works, and good things will flow.

We can do it, especially those of us in Africa and other underdeveloped parts of the world. For too long, we have been told we cannot succeed, but it is time for us to take our destiny into our own hands.

We need to JoyReP our lives by having fun, pursuing Ubuntu-driven relationships, finding flow, and living a life based on meaning. We need to follow the eight EntreHappiness Keys: mental fitness or mindset, meditation and nature, sleep, spirituality and faith, nutrition, hormesis, character, and physical fitness. We need grit, endurance, and a passion for our abundant future.

But most of all, we need to believe in ourselves and in our dreams. There is the inner game in you that remains to be unleashed, and only you can trigger that through the principles and models shared in this book. Take charge and define your destiny.

Our businesses deserve to take off. Our ideas deserve to impact the world. Our stories deserve to be told. Entrepreneurs make the world go round! The abundance and democratization of technologies have made it easier for the developing world to be able to catch up faster.

Where Am I Now?

I am in a good space with lots of joys, awesome relationships, work I love, and success defined by JoyReP. My success is about joy, calm, being present, family, and Happierspan. There are still bad days, but EntreHappiness strategies keep my energy high and my coping intact.

At Innolead, we have just partnered with young Motheo (twenty-four years old) and Mthabisi Bokete (thirty-one years old) for a start-up AI company called OrionX. We are all excited about the difference we will make for Africa in education and health.

In the past few years, my cancer diagnosis and the passing away of Mma Mmiga were devastating moments. Such will happen to anyone, and that is why resilience and grit become part of the arsenal for enduring entrepreneurs.

With the cancer, I got naturally scared that with all the enthusiasm I have about life, how could I depart so early? But I am doing well with treatments, and my happiness has long rebounded. I still miss Mma Mmiga, but the inheritance of virtues we got from her cheers me up.

My early years were tough as a start-up entrepreneur motivated by some wrong success factors like money and fame. If you are in that category of being young, full of energy, and bursting into entrepreneurship, restrain yourself from the damaging success-first mentality and chase your dreams based on the JoyReP formula for success.

I sometimes feel like I have lived multiple lives, having shown up in so many spaces: sports, choral music, dance group, farming, gardening, leadership, advising executives, family, friends, podcasting, overseas traveling, speaking, and now even learning how to play a guitar. And there is more to come! I now look forward to another fifty-five years with zest and enthusiasm. With longevity technologies and the science of happiness, it can be done.

As the first president of Botswana, Seretse Khama, said, "We should write our own history books to prove that we did have a past and that it was a past that was just as worth writing and learning about as any other."

Your story could touch the world if you will only let it be told. You may not come from a village in Botswana or somewhere else in Africa, but your unique past is worth learning about. Your family, your education, your passion, they all create who you are.

No one can impact the world quite like you can. Design your life, pursue your dreams, and challenge your status quo. Don't ever let anyone tell you what your path is going to be. The future is yours to create. Remember the song "My Way." You define your destiny!

The best stories are the ones lived fully, with joy, courage, and the belief that anything is possible. You will never embrace an unlimited future if you are too scared to make it your own. Conquer your fears, and embrace EntreHappiness and JoyReP. What's in your way is the way!

Transformation is in your hands. Happiness is a choice that is 110% an inside job!

We all have unique stories to share with the world. I have written my history book; it's time for you to write yours.

ENDNOTES

1   Sonja Lyubomirsky, Laura King, and Ed Diener, "The Benefits of Frequent Positive Affect: Does Happiness Lead to Success?," *Psychological Bulletin* 131, no. 6 (November 2005): 803–55, https://doi.org/10.1037/0033-2909.131.6.803.

2   "World Happiness Report 2024," The World Happiness Report, accessed March 29, 2025, https://worldhappiness.report/ed/2024/.

3   United Nations Conference on Trade and Development (UNCTAD), Science, Technology and Innovation Policy Review: Botswana (Geneva: UNCTAD), 2023, https://unctad.org/system/files/official-document/dtltikd2023d3_en.pdf.

4   "Botswana: Life Expectancy," World Health Organization, accessed March 29, 2025, https://data.who.int/countries/072.

5   Stephen E. Gilman et al., "Family Disruption in Childhood and Risk of Adult Depression," *American Journal of Psychiatry* 160, no. 5 (May 1, 2003): 939–46, https://doi.org/10.1176/appi.ajp.160.5.939.

6   Paul R. Amato, Sarah Patterson, and Brett Beattie, "Single-Parent Households and Children's Educational Achievement: A State-Level Analysis," *Social Science Research* 53 (September 2015): 191–202, https://doi.org/10.1016/j.ssresearch.2015.05.012.

7   "Debswana to Extend the Life of Botswana Diamond Production," De Beers Group, March 18, 2019, https://

www.debeersgroup.com/media/company-news/2019/
debswana-to-extend-life-of-botswana-diamond-production.

[8] *Guinness World Records, 2002* (New York, NY: Bantam Books, 2002).

[9] "Stoffel the Honeybadger," Legends and Legacies of Conservation in Africa, accessed April 7, 2025, https://legendsandlegaciesofafrica.org/stoffel.php.

[10] Martin E. P. Seligman, *Flourish: A Visionary New Understanding of Happiness and Well-Being* (New York, NY: Atria, 2013).

[11] "Joy," American Psychological Association, accessed April 7, 2025, https://dictionary.apa.org/joy.

[12] Robert W Smith, Julianne Holt-Lunstad, and Ichiro Kawachi, "Benchmarking Social Isolation, Loneliness, and Smoking: Challenges and Opportunities for Public Health," *American Journal of Epidemiology* 192, no. 8 (May 18, 2023): 1238–42, https://doi.org/10.1093/aje/kwad121.

[13] "Adult Development Study," Harvard Second Generation Study, accessed March 31, 2025, https://www.adultdevelopmentstudy.org/.

[14] "Stress in America 2022: Concerned for the Future, Beset by Inflation," American Psychological Association, October 20, 2022, https://www.apa.org/news/press/releases/stress/2022/concerned-future-inflation.

[15] Guro Engvig Løseth et al., "Stress Recovery with Social Support: A Dyadic Stress and Support Task," *Psychoneuroendocrinology* 146 (December 2022): 105949, https://doi.org/10.1016/j.psyneuen.2022.105949.

[16] Steven Kotler, "What Are Flow Triggers? 22 Examples to Unlock Flow State," Flow Research Collective - Leading Voice In Performance, August 23, 2023, https://www.flowresearchcollective.com/blog/flow-triggers.

17 Tony Robbins, *Money: Master the Game* (New York, NY: Simon & Schuster LTD, 2014).

18 "Table of Rankings," World Happiness Report 2023, accessed March 29, 2025, https://data.worldhappiness. report/table.

19 Blair T. Johnson and Rebecca L. Acabchuk, "What Are the Keys to a Longer, Happier Life? Answers from Five Decades of Health Psychology Research," *Social Science & Medicine* 196 (January 2018): 218–26, https://doi. org/10.1016/j.socscimed.2017.11.001.

20 Ed Diener and Micaela Y. Chan, "Happy People Live Longer: Subjective Well-Being Contributes to Health and Longevity," *Applied Psychology: Health and Well-Being* 3, no. 1 (January 27, 2011): 1–43, https://doi. org/10.1111/j.1758-0854.2010.01045.x.

21 Edmund Ruge, "Weber's Protestant Ethic Revisited: Explaining the Capitalism We Take for Granted - the Sais Review of International Affairs," The SAIS Review of International Affairs -, December 3, 2020, https://saisreview. sais.jhu.edu/return-to-max-vebers-theory-of-development.

22 Tom Rath and James K. Harter, *Wellbeing: The Five Essential Elements* (New York, NY: Gallup Press, 2014).

23 "Global Competitiveness Report 2020," World Economic Forum, accessed March 29, 2025, https://www.weforum.org/ publications/the-global-competitiveness-report-2020/.

24 "The Declaration of Independence, July 4, 1776," National Archives and Records Administration, accessed March 29, 2025, https://www.archives.gov/exhibits/american_originals/ declarat.html.

25 Sonja Lyubomirsky, Laura King, and Ed Diener, "The Benefits of Frequent Positive Affect: Does Happiness Lead to Success?," *Psychological Bulletin*

131, no. 6 (November 2005): 803–55, https://doi. org/10.1037/0033-2909.131.6.803.

26   "The 24 Character Strengths," VIA Institute On Character, accessed March 31, 2025, https://www.viacharacter.org/ character-strengths.

27   Sonja Lyubomirsky, "Subjective Happiness Scale," Positive Psychology Center, accessed March 29, 2025, https:// ppc.sas.upenn.edu/resources/questionnaires-researchers/ subjective-happiness-scale.

28   Barry M. Staw, Robert I. Sutton, and Lisa H. Pelled, "Employee Positive Emotion and Favorable Outcomes at the Workplace," *Organization Science* 5, no. 1 (February 1994): 51–71, https://doi.org/10.1287/orsc.5.1.51.

29   Tony Robbins.

30   Mark Hyman, "8 Simple Hacks for a Better Night's Sleep," Mark Hyman, MD, April 13, 2016, https://drhyman.com/ blogs/content/8-simple-hacks-for-a-better-nights-sleep.

31   K S Kendler, C O Gardner, and C A Prescott, "Religion, Psychopathology, and Substance Use and Abuse; a Multimeasure, Genetic-Epidemiologic Study," *American Journal of Psychiatry* 154, no. 3 (March 1, 1997): 322–29, https://doi.org/10.1176/ajp.154.3.322.

32   Mark Hyman, "The Good Type of Stress: Hormesis," Mark Hyman, MD, February 10, 2023, https://drhyman.com/ blogs/content/podcast-ep673.

33   David A. Sinclair, Matthew D. LaPlante, and Catherine Delphia, *Lifespan: Why We Age--and Why We Don't Have To* (New York, NY: Atria Books, 2019).

34   David Brooks, *The Road to Character* (New York, NY: Random House, 2016).

35   David C. Nieman and Laurel M. Wentz, "The Compelling Link between Physical Activity and the Body's Defense

System," *Journal of Sport and Health Science* 8, no. 3 (May 2019): 201–17, https://doi.org/10.1016/j.jshs.2018.09.009.

36 "Exercise: 7 Benefits of Regular Physical Activity," Mayo Clinic, August 26, 2023, https://www.mayoclinic.org/healthy-lifestyle/fitness/in-depth/exercise/art-20048389.

37 "Physical Activity and the Risk of Dementia," Alzheimer's Society, August 2024, https://www.alzheimers.org.uk/about-dementia/managing-the-risk-of-dementia/reduce-your-risk-of-dementia/physical-activity.

38 Jonas Nyabor, "Ghana's John Dumelo: The Actor Turned Farmer Champions Drive for Youth in Agriculture - the Africa Report.Com," The Africa Report, January 13, 2023, https://www.theafricareport.com/272523/ghanas-john-dumelo-the-actor-turned-farmer-champions-drive-for-youth-in-agriculture/.

39 Lovemore Mbigi and Jenny Maree, *Ubuntu: The Spirit of African Transformation Management* (Randburg, South Africa: Knowres Pub, 2005).

40 Madison Hoff, "The 25 Small and Midsize Companies with the Best Career Growth Opportunities," Business Insider, July 2022, https://www.businessinsider.com/comparably-small-midsize-companies-best-career-growth-opportunities-2022-7.

41 B Egolf et al., "The Roseto Effect: A 50-Year Comparison of Mortality Rates.," *American Journal of Public Health* 82, no. 8 (August 1992): 1089–92, https://doi.org/10.2105/ajph.82.8.1089.

42 Michael E. Porter and Nitin Nohria, "How CEOS Manage Time," Harvard Business Review, July 1, 2018, https://hbr.org/2018/07/how-ceos-manage-time.

43 Sonja Lyubomirsky, Kari L. Tucker, and Fazilet Kasri, "Responses to Hedonically Conflicting Social Comparisons: Comparing Happy and Unhappy People," *European Journal*

of Social Psychology 31, no. 5 (September 2001): 511–35, https://doi.org/10.1002/ejsp.82.

44 Marion Devaux and Franco Sassi, "Alcohol Consumption and Harmful Drinking: Trends And ...," OECD Health Working Papers, 2015, https://www.oecd.org/content/dam/oecd/en/publications/reports/2015/05/alcohol-consumption-and-harmful-drinking_g17a2638/5js1qwkz2p9s-en.pdf.

45 "Industry Statistics," National Drug-Free Workplace Alliance, November 14, 2023, https://www.ndwa.org/drug-free-workplace/industry-statistics/.

46 "Substance Abuse and Addiction Statistics [2023]," NCDAS, May 2, 2024, https://drugabusestatistics.org/.

47 Catherine Pearson, "How Many Friends Do You Really Need?," The New York Times, May 7, 2022, https://www.nytimes.com/2022/05/07/well/live/adult-friendships-number.html.

48 Scott Galloway, "Boys to Men," No Mercy / No Malice, July 21, 2023, https://www.profgalloway.com/boys-to-men/.

49 "From an Impoverished Single Mom to World's Richest Writer, a Look at JK Rowling's Incredible Journey - Creating Magic from Nothing," The Economic Times, July 31, 2023, https://economictimes.indiatimes.com/magazines/panache/from-an-impoverished-single-mom-to-worlds-richest-writer-a-look-at-jk-rowlings-incredible-journey/when-harry-potter-was-rejected-by-12-publishers/slideshow/102276515.cms?from=mdr.

50 Kenji Explains, "How Airbnb Founders Sold Cereal to Keep Their Dream Alive," Medium, August 15, 2020, https://ehandbook.com/how-airbnb-founders-sold-cereal-to-keep-their-dream-alive-d44223a9bdab.

51 Chris Nikic, "1% Better Challenge," Chris Nikic, accessed April 5, 2025, https://chrisnikic.com/1-percent-better.

52 Humphrey Carpenter, *J.R.R. Tolkien: A Biography* (London, UK: HarperCollinsPublishers, 2016).

53 Sughnen Yongo, "The 30 Greatest Book Series of All Time," Forbes, April 24, 2025, https://www.forbes.com/sites/entertainment/article/best-book-series/.

54 Suchayan Mandal, "Colonel Sanders Founded KFC at the Age of 65! Here's His Incredibly Inspiring Story | Business Insider India," Business Insider India, December 9, 2016, https://www.businessinsider.in/colonel-sanders-founded-kfc-at-the-age-of-65-heres-his-incrediblyinspiring-story/articleshow/55773640.cms.

55 "Oldest Graduate," Guinness World Records, May 26, 2016, https://www.guinnessworldrecords.com/world-records/oldest-graduate.

56 "How to Qualify," National Senior Games Association, accessed April 5, 2025, https://nsga.com/howtoqualify/.

57 LifeBank, accessed April 5, 2025, https://lifebankcares.com/.

58 "Ashish J. Thakkar | Unfoundation.Org," United Nations Foundation, accessed April 5, 2025, https://unfoundation.org/who-we-are/our-people/ashish-j-thakkar/.

59 "About Us," soleRebels, accessed April 5, 2025, https://www.solerebels.com/pages/about.

60 "About," Thione Niang, accessed April 5, 2025, https://thioneniang.com/about/.

51 "Deployments," Ushahidi, accessed April 5, 2025, https://www.ushahidi.com/in-action/deployments/.

ACKNOWLEDGMENTS

Every story begins somewhere—but mine would never have reached the page without the unwavering love and support of my family. To my wife, Nancy, your patience, encouragement, and belief in me are the quiet force behind everything I do. To my children, Tshepo, Motheo, Mbako, and Refilwe, thank you for being my everyday reminder of purpose. And to our grandchildren, Nakani, Chloe, Anjela-Joy, and Misha, you are the heartbeat of our family and the inspiration behind the decision to preserve this legacy in writing. This book is, in many ways, a love letter to you.

To the brilliant minds and generous souls at Innolead, our iTeam family, and the remarkable alumni who've contributed to a legacy five decades strong, thank you for co-authoring this journey with me. Your dedication made the Innolead story worth telling. To my business partners, Chilipi Mogasha and Okitanye Gaogane, thank you for your steadfast commitment and friendship. The journey would not be the same without your spirit, and I look forward to the chapters we've yet to write together.

To our ever-growing community at Innolead and the GrowthWell Podcast listeners, readers, guests, and collaborators, you've helped me stretch beyond the boardroom and into new realms of expression. Your feedback, your engagement, and your stories have fueled my own. You reminded me to keep showing up and to keep creating. *Ke nnile mooko o thata* you helped make me resilient.

To my coaching family at Strategic Coach—thank you for being a compass on my path since 2015. Dan Sullivan, your ideas lit the first spark of this book. And to my coach, Gary Matterstead, and the network of entrepreneurs who walk this journey alongside me, thank you for holding space for growth, clarity, and big dreams.

A very special thank you to Kary Oberbrunner and the incredible team at Ignite Souls, who carried this book with me through every high and low. You gave structure to my vision and strength to my voice.

To Wame Rasegakwana and Kutlo Wabepo Sedimo— thank you for being in the trenches with me, shaping the manuscript with care and crafting the messaging that brings this story to life. Your partnership has been nothing short of extraordinary.

This book may bear my name on the cover, but it was built by many hands, many hearts, and many voices. Thank you for helping me tell this story. Thank you for being part of it.

ABOUT THE AUTHOR

Oabona Michael Kgengwenyane founded Innolead Consulting, DigitalGae Technologies, and Manenzo Farming. For over 20 years, he has advised businesses and entrepreneurs on how to manage their companies efficiently and effectively. He has been a guest speaker at international events such as the Engineering Institute of Zambia Conference and the 2004 JCI World Congress.

Oabona exited the corporate world in 1999 when joining the entrepreneurial world, driven by passion to impact lives through insights and ideas. He has grown Innolead to be the largest and leading consulting firm in Botswana (staff of 60) that is home-grown with presence in other African countries like Zambia, Uganda, and Rwanda. The company has supported blue-chip organizations with world-class solutions in digital transformation, project management, corporate strategy, and organizational transformation for over 20 years. Connect more at InnoLeadAfrica.com and oabona.com

CONNECT
WITH OABONA

Follow him on your favorite
social media platforms today.

Oabona.com

GROWTH WELL PODCAST

Growthwell podcast is dedicated to exploring impactful ideas and insights that foster positive psycho-socio-economic growth across Africa.

At Growth Well, we engage in thought-provoking discussions, interviews, and stories that inspire our listeners to cultivate growth in their communities. The concept of "growth" symbolizes progress and development, while "well" reflects the nurturing essence of water wells, a vital part of African culture.

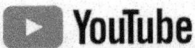

▶ YouTube   Spotify